Law Librarianship in Academic Libraries

CHANDOS
INFORMATION PROFESSIONAL SERIES
Series Editor: Ruth Rikowski
(email: Rikowskigr@aol.com)

Chandos' new series of books is aimed at the busy information professional. They have been specially commissioned to provide the reader with an authoritative view of current thinking. They are designed to provide easy-to-read and (most importantly) practical coverage of topics that are of interest to librarians and other information professionals. If you would like a full listing of current and forthcoming titles, please visit www.chandospublishing.com.

New authors: we are always pleased to receive ideas for new titles; if you would like to write a book for Chandos, please contact Dr Glyn Jones on g.jones.2@elsevier.com or telephone +44 (0) 1865 843000.

Law Librarianship in Academic Libraries

Best Practices

Yemisi Dina

AMSTERDAM • BOSTON • HEIDELBERG • LONDON
NEW YORK • OXFORD • PARIS • SAN DIEGO
SAN FRANCISCO • SINGAPORE • SYDNEY • TOKYO

Chandos Publishing is an imprint of Elsevier

Chandos Publishing is an imprint of Elsevier
225 Wyman Street, Waltham, MA 02451, USA
Langford Lane, Kidlington, OX5 1GB, UK

Notices
Knowledge and best practice in this field are constantly changing. As new research and
experience broaden our understanding, changes in research methods, professional practices,
or medical treatment may become necessary.

Practitioners and researchers must always rely on their own experience and knowledge in
evaluating and using any information, methods, compounds, or experiments described herein.
In using such information or methods they should be mindful of their own safety and the safety
of others, including parties for whom they have a professional responsibility.

To the fullest extent of the law, neither the Publisher nor the authors, contributors, or editors,
assume any liability for any injury and/or damage to persons or property as a matter of products
liability, negligence or otherwise, or from any use or operation of any methods, products,
instructions, or ideas contained in the material herein.

ISBN: 978-0-08-100144-8

British Library Cataloguing-in-Publication Data
A catalogue record for this book is available from the British Library

Library of Congress Cataloging-in-Publication Data
A catalog record for this book is available from the Library of Congress

Library of Congress Control Number: 2015932039

For information on all Chandos Publishing publications
visit our website at http://store.elsevier.com/

Working together
to grow libraries in
developing countries

www.elsevier.com • www.bookaid.org

Dedication

This book is dedicated to:

the memory of my parents who made my education
possible even when they were not around;
to my husband Adekunle Dina who made law librarianship
possible with his support and advice;
to my children Demi, Dami and Dasola who continue
to endure the journey with me;
to All who believed in me
and helped make things happen.

Contents

List of figures and tables

About the author

Yemisi Dina is a law librarian with extensive experience working in academic law libraries. She is currently an Associate Librarian/Head of Public Services at the Osgoode Hall Law School Library, York University, Toronto, Canada. As an active member of professional law library associations she has participated at their conferences, meetings and professional development activities. She is a recipient of the Janine Miller Fellowship of the Canadian Association of Law Libraries and the Canadian Legal Information Institute.

Acknowledgement

The author will like to acknowledge the following individuals and organizations:

1. American Association of Law Libraries
2. British & Irish Association of Law Libraries
3. Canadian Association of Law Libraries
4. Chartered Institute of Libraries and Information Professionals
5. Mr. Tom Arban (Tom Arban Photography, Toronto, Canada)
6. Mr. F. Tim Knight (Associate Librarian/Head of Technical Services, Osgoode Hall Law School, Toronto, Canada)
7. Ms Janice Modeste (Law Librarian, Hugh Wooding Law School Library, Trinidad & Tobago)
8. Mr. Sadri Saieb (Head Librarian, Swiss Institute of Comparative Law, Lausanne, Switzerland)
9. Ms Virginia Corner (Manager, Communications, Osgoode Hall Law School, Toronto, Canada)

Prologue

The five laws of library science
Books are for use
Every reader his [or her] book
Every book its reader
Save the reader time
The library is a growing organism
                    S. R. Ranganathan

Libraries are reservoirs of strength, grace and wit, reminders of order, calm, and continuity, lakes of mental energy, neither warm nor cold, light nor dark in any library in the world, I am at home, unselfconscious, still and absorbed.

Germaine Greer

Introduction

Law librarianship is an area of specialization in librarianship. While training to become a librarian, courses are taught within a short period on legal information resources but not much is said about the practices and what to expect. This book is a guide for librarians who want to pursue a career in academic law libraries. It provides basic information on the best practices in academic law libraries and serves as a guide for library school students by detailing what they can expect if they choose to work in a law library.

What is law librarianship?

Law librarianship is a specialized field in the practice of librarianship. Librarians with this focus work and practice in law libraries belonging to academic institutions, government departments and agencies such as the Attorney General's office, Courthouses, law firms and legislative or special libraries.

Qualifications for law librarians

Unlike the legal profession, Law Librarians do not have licensing and regulatory bodies that review the standards for the profession. However, in some countries such as the United Kingdom and Nigeria there are regulatory bodies for the librarianship profession. This is discussed later in this chapter. It is common to find that law librarians have university degrees in law and Masters in Library Science. This is very common in many academic and government law libraries in the United States and Canada. There has been a lot of discussions as to whether or not a librarian working in a law library needs a dual degree. Each country has its own standards, expectations and practices that have also been influenced by a number of factors over the years such as finances, work experience, institutional standards, hiring practices, accreditation requirements and other professional training options.

While obtaining a law degree is not mandatory for anyone who wants to work in law libraries, it will always be of great benefit when carrying out professional duties. In the academic law library, one advantage of having a law degree is that it gives that person a proper understanding and knowledge of the materials in a law collection as well as an understanding of student and faculty expectations. From a practical point of view, Demers (2012) noted the usefulness of a law degree, especially when answering questions at the reference desk.

Similarly, the knowledge of foreign, comparative and international law (FCIL) is emerging as a requirement for law librarians applying to work in academic law libraries. Law librarians in this position are referred to as FCIL librarians and this is a common practice and trend in many law schools in the United States. An FCIL librarian is familiar with the laws and practices of one or more jurisdictions in a region. For example, such a librarian may be knowledgeable in Asian laws in which case they may know about the laws of China, Korea, Indonesia, Malaysia or other countries in that continent. Or an FCIL librarian responsible for the Caribbean will likely understand the laws of most countries in that region such as Trinidad & Tobago, Jamaica, Barbados etc. These librarians usually understand the legal systems of multiple jurisdictions. Knowledge of international law means an understanding of the role and concepts of international law and an understanding of the practices of international organizations such as the United Nations and its organs. Researchers and professors outside of the law school but within the university rely on the expertise and knowledge of FCIL librarians when they need information about other foreign jurisdictions.

Another emerging requirement for academic law librarians is fluency in languages other than English such as French, Spanish, German, Italian and Chinese. Many academic law libraries' job postings have indicated the requirement of fluency in these languages lately. One explanation for requiring the knowledge of a foreign language may be the global trend in law practice for foreign trade with emerging markets. Lawyers and legal researchers need information from foreign jurisdictions that will likely be available in the foreign language. A librarian who understands and can translate the information will naturally be a useful member of the team. Rumsey, a highly respected foreign, comparative and international law librarian in the United States observed that: "Historically, French, German, Spanish and Italian have been the most common languages used by FCIL librarians. With increasing legal and financial interest in China, however, knowledge of Chinese might be even more marketable."

Gaining a dual degree may be an expensive venture, but from a practical point of view, and from my experience, a law degree always comes in very handy and is extremely useful when working in an academic law library. As an administrator in an academic law library, you come into contact with other administrators and academics in the faculty; the knowledge of the law elevates the status and that helps to command some respect from faculty members and students. Note that this does infer that those Law Librarians without a law degree do not command any respect from the academic community.

A law librarian with the dual degree understands the language of the profession and its nuances. For example, this background is helpful for understanding the "territorial" attitude of law students. In all the institutions in which I have worked I have come to the conclusion that this attitude is the same globally. Law students love their space and don't enjoy seeing non-law students studying there even if they are genuinely there for academic purposes. I remember that when I was in law school, the law library was exclusively located in the basement of the university library but it had the level of comfort that an undergraduate could wish for; it was very obvious that other students in the university were not welcome at this location!

Understanding this cultural difference will help administrators when planning services for the academic law library. This will equip them with a broader understanding of user needs when creating library policies related to seating, readers services among others.

The following are some of the educational qualification practices of librarians working in academic law libraries in Canada, United States, United Kingdom, South Africa, The Caribbean and Nigeria:

Canada

In Canada, many of the law library directors in Canadian law schools have a degree in law and librarianship. (Seven of the directors have dual degrees i.e. law degrees and a master's degree in library science). The Canadian Association of Law Libraries is a professional membership body of law libraries in Canada. This body is not a licensing or regulatory body and so they do not have any required qualifications for law librarians. The executive board of the Canadian Association of Law Libraries (CALL) is in the process of developing and creating its competencies for law librarianship.

The standards of accreditation for law schools in Canada are different from that of the United States; but there is no requirement about the educational qualification of law librarians.

United States

The American Association of Law Libraries (AALL) is the professional organization in the United States responsible for providing the promotion and advancement of law libraries. The AALL is a membership organization with about 5,000 members. Similar to Canada, the organization is not a licensing body. However, the Career website on educational requirements for the law librarianship profession, the American Association of Law Libraries stated that the majority of law librarians have a graduate degree in library and information science but the requirement for a law degree depends on the institution. Nevertheless, there are some libraries that have lawyers and attorneys without a law degree working in their institutions.

The American Association of Law Libraries (AALL) has defined the law librarianship profession by creating a list of competencies for members of this profession based on "knowledge, skills, abilities and personal characteristics". The list of these competencies are available here - http://www.aallnet.org/main-menu/Publications/spectrum/Archives/Vol-5/pub_sp0106/pub-sp0106-comp.pdf.

The AALL competencies are widely acknowledged and practiced all over the world and have been used for recruitment and promotion purposes. The competencies are divided into Core and Specialized areas which are acquired at different stages of one's career. The Core competencies are more general, apply to everyone and will have been acquired early in one's career. I have decided to highlight the following skills:

- Strong commitment to excellent client service
- Recognizing the diverse nature of a library's client
- Understanding the culture and context of the parent institution
- Demonstrating knowledge of the legal system and the legal profession
- Exhibiting leadership skills, regardless of position within management structure
- Exhibiting understanding of a multidisciplinary and cross-functional approach to programs and projects within the organization
- Recognizing the value of professional networking and participating in professional associations
- Actively pursuing personal and professional growth through continuing education.

The above are critical benchmarks that every professional law librarian should refer to at the beginning of their career and periodically check their progress and advancement in line with these requirements. There is no identification of the number of years that counts as early career but from my experience a professional should have been able to build and develop all these competencies in the first eight years of working in this field.

The Specialized competencies are skills required for different areas of specialization and have been divided into:

1. Library Management,
2. Reference, Research and Client Services
3. Information Technology
4. Collection Care and Management
5. Teaching

These are library-related areas and it has been acknowledged that it is possible for a librarian to be specialized or have responsibilities in more than one of these areas.

Many law librarians that I have interacted with in North America have built their careers in line with these competencies regardless of whether or not they have dual degrees.

Standard 603(C) of the American Bar Association standards for Approved Law Schools states that: "The director of a law library should have a law degree and a degree in library or information science and shall have a sound knowledge of and experience in library administration". Using this requirement a number of law schools in the United States strive to follow this criteria when making appointments and this can be clarified from job advertisements posted on the job site of various law schools and on the website of the American Association of Law Libraries.

United Kingdom

Law librarians in the United Kingdom are classified among legal information professionals according to a publication of the British & Irish Association of Law Librarians (BIALL). The main qualifications suggested for entry to the profession are either an undergraduate or postgraduate degree in librarianship and information studies noting that "a law degree may be an advantage but not essential". The BIALL as a professional association continuously organizes training sessions on legal information sources for its members and other interested parties. The Chartered Institute of Librarians and Information Professionals (CILIP) is responsible for promoting and supporting the librarianship profession in the United Kingdom.

Law schools in the United Kingdom are guided by a set of comprehensive and flexible standards created by the Society of Legal Scholars. These standards provide guidance on the provision of services, staffing, management, resource, access, delivery policies, equipment and building. They are reviewed periodically based on surveys sent out to law schools through the British and Irish Association of Law Libraries. Standard 1.3 states that it is desirable that a law librarian should hold a legal qualification. However, in the results of the survey for 2007/8, 75% of university libraries in the United Kingdom did not meet this requirement.

The Caribbean

The Caribbean in this context represents the English-speaking territories: namely, Antigua, The Bahamas, Barbados, Belize, The British Virgin Islands, The Cayman Islands, Dominica, Grenada, Guyana, Jamaica, Montserrat, St Kitts and Nevis, St Lucia, St Vincent, Trinidad and Tobago, The Turks and Caicos. There are no strict requirements for the qualification of law librarians in these countries. In the Faculty of Law, University of The West Indies, Cave Hill, Barbados, the head of the library past and present both have law degrees. Similarly, at the Council of Legal Education libraries in Trinidad, Jamaica and The Bahamas, there are no strict requirements for a law degree but past and current librarians have dual degrees.

The Department of Library & Information Studies, University of the West Indies (UWI) offers undergraduate and graduate programs in library and information studies for librarians in the Caribbean. Historically, many law librarians from the Caribbean studied in the United Kingdom, United States and Canada.

South Africa

The Organisation of South African Law Libraries http://www.osall.org.za/ is the national law library organization. One of its objectives is: "To enhance and develop the practice of law librarianship and provide opportunities for professional growth for law librarians and training for those who work with legal materials in libraries or information centres in South Africa". Many of the library schools provide training for library school students who want to specialize in law librarianship.

Nigeria

In Nigeria there are two organizations that are responsible for the accreditation of law programs offered in universities. They are the Council of Legal Education and the National Universities Commission. Both organizations require that the head of an academic law library must have a Masters degree in Library Science as well as a degree in law and they must have been called to the Nigerian Bar. Note, however, that everyone who is practicing as a librarian in Nigeria must have passed through the chartership process through the Librarians Registration Council of Nigeria (LRCN). The Nigerian Association of Law Libraries is the professional membership body responsible for leadership and promotion of law libraries, but they do not have any firm requirements for the education of law librarians. The Nigerian Library Association coordinates the activities of all libraries and librarians in Nigeria; this body does not have any specific educational qualifications for law librarians. Similarly there is the Librarians Registration Council of Nigeria (LRCN), a body created by the Federal Government of Nigeria whose mandate is to determine the standards and skills of chartered librarians. The LRCN does not have any clear requirements for the qualification of law librarians.

Education of law librarians

Librarians working in the law library attend library school to attain professional library degrees, usually a graduate degree Master of Library & Information Science (Studies) MLIS, MLS, MISt; but note that the names and acronyms varies depending on the awarding institutions. A very common practice in many countries is for librarians to study librarianship and eventually opt to study law along the line. But the history of academic law librarianship in the United States is the opposite as law students were some of the first group of persons to be hired to manage law libraries, which means that they did not initially have any librarianship qualifications. In the past two decades, the experience has been vice-versa with practicing lawyers/attorneys going back to library school and embracing law librarianship as a second career. Law graduates are also finishing law school and going back for graduate studies in library science.

Education for law librarians has evolved over the years from just acquiring skills in librarianship. Some library schools now have combined programs that qualify persons immediately upon graduation to work in a law library; dual programs are now available in law faculties and library schools in the United States and Canada. Students who enroll in such programs graduate with a Masters in Library and Information Science and a Juris Doctor (equivalent of LL.B in Commonwealth countries). In the early 1970s having a dual degree was the trend and was a great advantage for those who had them. Berring (2013) noted that in the United States in 1975 the profession of law librarianship was ablaze as newer law schools were being set up and the older generation of law library directors were retiring so having a dual degree created opportunities and was a gateway for advancing quickly in this career. See Appendix 2 for a list of dual programs in Canada and the United States.

Academic law libraries

The academic law library exists to meet the research and teaching needs of students and faculty and in some instances members of the public; but the primary patrons are students and faculty. This means that the services provided will accommodate the needs of this clientele. The collection will be developed and built to facilitate and enhance teaching and research of faculty and students.

Structure of academic law libraries

The administrative reporting structure in academic law libraries remains a contentious and debatable issue all over the world. The most common ones are autonomous and centralized structures. Some law libraries are independent of the main university library while some function directly under the university library. Where the law library is autonomous, the head of the law library reports to the Dean of the Law School and the library budget and administration are managed through them.

This is very common in law schools in the United States. Under the centralized system, the law library functions under the main library, the head of the law library reports to the Dean of Libraries/University Librarian or to the Associate University Librarian who is in charge of unit libraries and the budget is administered through that office. In instances where the law collection sits within the main university library among other subjects there is usually a librarian designated to manage this collection who reports to the Dean of Libraries/University Librarian. In some institutions, the head of the law library reports to both the Dean of the Law School and the Dean of Libraries/University Librarian. This structure exists in the Cornell University Law Library, University of Buffalo Law Library and the Vanderbilt Law Library.

One of the benefits of an autonomous law library is the assurance that the library will receive more financial support from the law school especially from donations that are received from alumni, law firms and other corporations. In many of the jurisdictions where I have worked and practiced as a law librarian, there is the general assumption that the legal profession is elitist and its members are wealthy so the law school will likely receive more substantial donations, gifts and endowments than other areas of an institution.

In the ABA Standards for Approval of Law Schools 2013–2014 there is a preference for an autonomous structure, especially in terms of managing the growth and development of the law library. See Standard 602 - http://www.americanbar.org/content/dam/aba/publications/misc/legal_education/Standards/2013_2014_standards_chapter6.authcheckdam.pdf.

Under the centralized system, the university library distributes the funds and resources equally among all the departmental and unit libraries. Equal distribution may be fair and equitable but the cost of law materials makes this an impracticable option that usually causes a lot of friction between university management and the head of the law library. Nevertheless, in a centralized system, the law library may be treated like any other branch library. And if the library is located within the law outside the main library; the distance tends to isolate the staff from others in the centralized system. From my experience, the partnership between the stakeholders in the centralized system requires a great sense of understanding and the willingness to collaborate when making financial decisions.

The library building is usually situated on the grounds or the same facility as the law school, especially where they are autonomous from the main university library. One advantage of this is that it provides exclusive access to the library facility for law faculty and students.

There have been many criticisms of both structures and decisions are usually made by the university administration based on accreditation standards. In the United States, many of the academic law libraries follow the standards required by the accreditation bodies. Price (1960) noted the disparity between an autonomous and centralized system: "The principal stigmata of the so-called "autonomous" law school library are closer budget control by the law school, hiring and discharge of library personnel, and book-selection autonomy. It is in the discussions of the exercise of these functions, as between director and dean that the most significant analytical fallacies occur.... With a library-minded dean, conscious of the place of the law library in his scheme of things and willing to fight for it, success within budget limitations is almost assured under either system. On the other hand, if the dean is indifferent to the library needs, or weak, the autonomous library is a mess (and for every unsatisfactory law library in a centralized system, I can show you an autonomous law library just as bad). Contrariwise, in a centralized system, the law library may or may not be a stepchild, depending upon how enlightened the director is and how willing he is to cooperate in solving the peculiar problems of the law library."

Price's observation continues to exist and dominate many academic law libraries, which means that library directors need a lot of tact and a high sense of professionalism in tackling these issues. Many law schools have competing needs for the limited budget so it will take a dean who is library-centric and focused to clearly articulate the financial needs of the library in their planning.

Milles (2004) suggested that there are varying models that academic law libraries can apply: "Law schools exist largely, but not solely, to train lawyers for private practice and public interest work. Law libraries exist to serve that goal. The autonomy of the law library must be viewed as a means toward achieving that goal, not an end in itself. Consideration must be given to the ways in which autonomous decision-making serves those goals, as well as the ways in which cooperation and collaboration contribute to meeting those needs. It no longer makes sense to insist on the dualistic conception of law libraries as either autonomous or branch libraries, ignoring the range of shading in between.

"Developments and trends such as availability of electronic legal resources and increasing multidisciplinary approach to legal research calls for academic libraries to rethink the structuring of libraries from autonomous and centralized systems."

Table 1.1 below is a sample list of the structure of academic law libraries in the United States, United Kingdom, Canada, The Caribbean and Nigeria. The selected libraries are publicly funded institutions except for the United States which is a combination of public and private.

Table 1.1 Examples of administrative structure in academic law libraries

Autonomous	Centralized
United States	
Harvard Law School Library Lillian Goldman Law Library, Yale University Cornell Law University Law Library Robert Crown Law Library, Stanford University Arthur W. Diamond Law Library, Columbia Law School New York University Law Library	D'Angelo Law Library, University of Chicago

(*Continued*)

Table 1.1 (Continued)

Autonomous	Centralized
University of Michigan Law Library University of Minnesota Law Library University of Iowa Law Library	
Both	
Cornell Law University Law Library	University of Buffalo Law Library
Canada	
Osgoode Hall Law School Library, York University Bora Laskin Law Library, University of Toronto Sir James Dunn Law Library, Dalhousie University Brian Dickson Law Libraries, University of Ottawa Law Library, University of Moncton Université de Laval Law Library, Thompson Rivers University Paul Martin Law Library, University of Windsor	Nahum Gelber Law Library, McGill University Lederman Law Library, Queens University John A. Weir Memorial Law Library, University of Alberta University of British Columbia Law Library Bennett Jones Law Library, University of Calgary E.K. Williams Law Library, University of Manitoba Gerard V.la Forest Law Library, University of New Brunswick Law Library, University of Saskatchewan Diana M. Priestly Law Library, University of Victoria John & Dotsa Bitove Family Law Library, Western University
United Kingdom	
	Bodlcian Law Library, Oxford University Squire Law Library, University of Cambridge University of Cardiff
Caribbean	
Faculty of Law, University of The West Indies	College of The Bahamas Law Library
Nigeria	
	Adeola Odutola Law Library, University of Ibadan Law Library, University of Lagos Law Library, Obafemi Awolowo University, Ile-Ife Law Library, Ahmadu Bello University Law Library, Ogun State University

History of academic law libraries

Academic law libraries have evolved from the collection of practicing lawyers as many law school libraries were created from book donations from the libraries of these individuals. In the United States the foundation of larger institutionalized law library collection in the 19th and 20th century was developed from books in the private collections of lawyers. Roy Mersky recalled that the Founders Collection at the Yale Law Library is made up of the collections of Seth P. Staples, Samuel J. Hitchcock and David Daggett; while Edward C. Kent donated his collection to Columbia Law Library in 1911; Cornell acquired collections of Merrett King (1886) and Nathaniel Moak (1893).

In the United Kingdom, the oldest academic law library is the Bodleian Law Library at Oxford University, it originated from an endowment from Duke Humphrey. Jeffries (1989) recalled that the academic institutions collected law books but there were no librarians as the position was not treated as a professional but janitorial one.

Canadian law school libraries have also been managed by administrators who were not librarians but who had legal backgrounds. However, the oldest academic law library in this jurisdiction was established by a distinguished and respected law librarian whose collection development skills created a leading collection in the Commonwealth. One of the early donations to the Osgoode Hall Law School library came from the estate of the late Phillips Stewart, a law student who died before he could complete his education but gave a substantial amount which was endowed specifically for buying books for the library. This endowment is still being used for this purpose.

In Nigeria, many of the academic institutions were established after its independence from Great Britain. During the colonial administration, the common practice was for students to travel to the United Kingdom for their education. However, after 1960, it became necessary to train lawyers in local laws. The Faculty of Law, University of Nigeria, Nsukka is the oldest which includes a law library. This library and those of the first generation universities such as University of Lagos, Obafemi Awolowo University (formerly University of Ife) don't have separate law libraries; the law collection is part of the main university library. The Faculty of Law at the University of Ibadan was the last to be established among the first generation universities; its library is situated on the grounds of the law school but it is centrally-administered by the main university library. The law library building in Ibadan is a donation from the estate of Nigeria's prominent industrialist, the late Chief T. Adeola Odutola, and the building is named after him.

Accreditation & standards for academic law libraries

Just like other professional courses such as medicine, dentistry etc., the regulatory bodies responsible for the legal profession in some jurisdictions around the world require that law libraries meet certain standards before the law school program is approved. The essence of accreditation is to ensure that the institutions provide adequate and appropriate resources for the programs being offered. Libraries should provide all the resources to support teaching, learning and research. The accreditation exercise involves site visits to the different institutions by a selected team, which always includes librarians. In the United States, United Kingdom, Canada and Nigeria; the regulatory bodies have specific requirements that must be met before law programs can be approved. In the Caribbean, each country has its own standards and requirements; I have outlined below those of Barbados, Jamaica and Trinidad and Tobago.

In Trinidad and Tobago, the Accreditation Council of Trinidad and Tobago Act established the body that is responsible for "conducting and advising on the accreditation and recognition of post-secondary (sic) and tertiary educational and training institutions, programmes and awards, whether local or foreign, and for the promotion of the quality and standards". The Accreditation Council is responsible for the quality assurance and accreditation of professional courses being offered in tertiary institutions in that country. More information is available on their website here - http://www.actt.org.tt/index.php/services/accreditation.

The relevant institutions are the Faculty of Law Library, University of The West Indies, St. Augustine campus.

The University Council of Jamaica is responsible for national quality assurance in Jamaica. The relevant institution is the Faculty of Law Library, Mona Campus. More information about the organization is available here - http://www.ucj.org.jm/content/what-accreditation-0.

The Barbados Accreditation Council was established by the Barbados Accreditation Council Act of 2004 to provide registration, accreditation and related services in post-secondary and tertiary institutions in Barbados. The Faculty of Law, Cave Hill Campus, Barbados falls under the jurisdiction of the Barbados Accreditation Council. More information about the Council is available here - http://www.bac.gov.bb/Accreditation.htm.

In Nigeria, there are two institutions that are responsible for the accreditation of law schools:

1. Council of Legal Education
2. Nigerian Universities Commission (NUC) http://www.nuc.edu.ng/pages/pages.asp?id=27

The Nigerian Universities Commission is an arm of the Federal Ministry of Education. One of its mandates is "to ensure quality assurance of all academic programmes offered in Nigerian universities". Every five years, the Commission's Quality Assurance team conducts accreditation site visits to public and private institutions evaluating their resources, equipment and facilities to ensure that they meet the standards required to facilitate the different programmes.

The Council of Legal Education is the body responsible for the training and regulation of the legal profession in Nigeria; they also manage the schools where practical training is offered after undergraduate legal education. This body is responsible for the accreditation and approval of law programs in public and private universities in Nigeria. They evaluate law programmes by conducting site visits and

they have their own standard requirements which must be met before any law pro-
gramme can be offered in universities. The Council of Legal Education provides a
list of materials which are required for any academic law library in Nigeria. These
are the items that will be during site visits to institutions.

United States

The American Bar Association (ABA) and the Association of American Law
Schools (AALS) are the two organizations responsible for the regulation of the
legal education in the United States. The ABA standards are reviewed and updated
annually and are available here — http://www.americanbar.org/groups/legal_
education/resources/standards.html.

Byelaw 6 (8) of the AALS states as follows:

a. A member school shall maintain a library adequate to support and encourage the instruction and research of its faculty and students. A law library of a member school shall pos-
   sess or have ready access to a physical collection and other information resources that
   substantially:
   i.   meet the research needs of its students, satisfy the demands of its curricular offerings,
        particularly in those respects in which student research is expected, and allows for the
        training of its students in the use of various research methodologies;
   ii. support the individual research interests of its faculty members;
   iii. serve any special research and educational objectives expressed by the school or
        implicit in its chosen role in legal education.
b. The library is an integral part of the law school and shall be organized and administered
   to perform its educational function and to assure a high standard of service.
c. A member school shall have a full-time librarian and a staff of sufficient number and
   with sufficient training to develop and maintain a high level of service to the program.

http://www.aals.org/about_handbook_bylaws.php.

There are other accreditation bodies for post-secondary and tertiary institutions
but I have chosen to focus on the ones relevant to academic law libraries. The standards of accreditation in law schools in the United States is a long standing and
established practice. Many countries like Nigeria have designed and structured their
accreditation standards against the American model considering its consistency
over the years.

United Kingdom

In the United Kingdom, the Society of Legal Scholars came up with a Statement of
Standards for University Law Library Provision which serves as a guide for the
operation of an academic law library. They were drawn from the opinion and contributions of legal scholars, law librarians and government bodies. These standards
are updated following the trends of activities in academic law libraries in the
United Kingdom in the form of a survey which is conducted by members of the
British and Irish Association of Law Librarians. They contain requirements for minimum holdings for a law library that take into consideration the number of students

at the undergraduate and postgraduate levels, development in the publication format (print versus electronic), curriculum changes etc. The list of materials in the standards serves as guidance for law library administrators in building their collection. There was a major revision of the Statement in 2009 as a result of major developments in legal education and "Particular attention was paid to the balance between print and electronic sources of information, remote access to information resources and services, the use of wireless technology, the relative roles of the library and the law school in teaching research skills, the growing incorporation of information literacy objectives, the comprehensive collection statements, and the standards for franchising and distance learning."

Note that the Statement is not an accreditation tool; there are other bodies responsible for the accreditation of higher education and tertiary institutions in the United Kingdom.

Canada

The Federation of Law Societies of Canada is responsible for the regulation of the legal profession in Canada. This body does not have any guidelines or standards exclusively for academic law libraries except in a recent document prepared by a task force set up in June 2007. As part of the requirements for a new law school in the Task Force recommendations: "The law school maintains a law library in electronic and/or paper form that provides services and collections sufficient in quality and quantity to permit the law school to foster and attain its teaching, learning and research objectives". This is the closest standard required for academic law libraries in Canada, and there are no other requirements for the position of law librarians or library directors. It is usually left to the institutions to decide.

There are provincial quality assurance bodies that facilitate accreditation of higher education in Canada; for example there is the Ontario Universities Council on Quality Assurance which is responsible for assuring the quality of all publicly funded university programs and overseeing the regular audit of each university's quality assurance processes.

There also exists a set of standards prepared by the Canadian Academic Law Library Directors – Canadian Academic Law Library Standards (2007).

Chapter 6 explains in detail the standards required for library and information resources with respect to library collection and law librarian positions.

It should be noted that some institutions have chosen to ignore some of the required standards and have been able to survive, which leads one to question whether it is still relevant to have such rigorous exercises. Accreditation standards have been described as a toothless but bothersome dog by Berry (2013).

I had the opportunity to participate in two successful accreditation visits by both the Council for Legal Education and the NUC while working at the Adeola Odutola Law Library, University of Ibadan, Nigeria. Both exercises were very intense but the law library was ranked as one of the very strong areas of the law school.

Other types of law libraries

Court house

The court house libraries are established to serve the courts. The courts in any jurisdiction are at different levels and in most countries the Supreme Court is the highest
court. Each court has its own library and the collection is mainly for the use of the
judges and sometimes to members of the legal profession. Most court libraries are
not open to the public with the library residing within the court premises. Many of
these courts provide excellent document delivery services as well as maintain an
updated website with useful information. See Appendix for a list of courts in some
Commonwealth countries and the United States.

Attorney-general's office

The Attorney-General's Office is also known as the Ministry of Justice in some jurisdictions. The libraries are set up for the use of government lawyers. Depending on
the jurisdiction, each state or province has its own library and there is one assigned
to the federal level. This is the practice in Canada, United Kingdom, Nigeria, The
Bahamas, Barbados, and Trinidad and Tobago.

Legislative

Legislative libraries are found in the parliaments of most countries. This type of
library is established for the use of members of the legislative assembly and their
research assistants. They are not open to members of the public. The Library of
Congress and the Library of Parliament, Canada, are examples of legislative
libraries.

Law firms

The library in a law firm is set up to meet the needs of legal practitioners in private
practice. Depending on the size of the law practice it is not uncommon to find very
large law libraries to facilitate legal research or just a small collection for a solo
practitioner. In cases where it is a very large practice with law offices in different
parts of a country or the world, the library will tend to share its resources. These
libraries are strictly for private use and are not open to the public.

Special libraries

The collections in these types of libraries are mostly for research. Examples are the
Nigerian Institute of Advanced Legal Studies, Institute of Advanced Legal Studies,
London and the Swiss Institute of Comparative Law. These libraries are for the use
of researchers affiliated with these institutions while visiting researchers are
provided access by request.

Conclusion

Law libraries are an essential tool for the training of potential legal practitioners and it is necessary to require that they are properly and adequately maintained. This chapter has discussed the history of academic law libraries, the education and training of law librarians who are the essentials who manage the functions and operations of the library, the administrative structures that exist in law libraries and future recommendations.

Users of the academic law library

2

Understanding the types of users who use the academic law library promotes efficiency in the management and administration of the unit. It is very important to have a knowledge of user categories. The law librarian should be able to identify the different categories of users who are using the collection and the library space. The following constitute the groups of users who patronize an academic law library:

1. Faculty/Professors (Full-time & Adjunct)
2. Graduate students (LL.M & PhD)
3. Undergraduate students (JD/LL.B)
4. Distance education students
5. Researchers
6. Visiting fellows
7. Users with disabilities
8. Mooting teams
9. Law Journal editors
10. Alumni
11. Members of the public

Faculty/Professors (Full-time & Adjunct)

Full-time faculty members are the major consumers of library services and resources; they use and consult library materials for their teaching and research. Many of them maintain a good rapport with librarians and library staff and some often know their way around the space. You will often find them coming to browse the new periodicals or retrieving books from the library by themselves. They are also interested in knowing about the newly acquired publications and resources that have been added to the library's collection periodically.

Adjunct faculty members teach on a part-time basis. They are usually legal practitioners who are supporting and helping to enhance the experiential skills of students; or they may even be teaching in other law schools.

Faculty members at all levels rely on library resources for preparing their research and teaching materials so it is important that the library provide them with current materials as and when necessary. Some of them will ask for a librarian's assistance to create and maintain their course websites by checking for the latest editions of course readings, updates on topical legal issues, legislation and case law. Lewis (2002) observed that there is a varying culture among law school professors' interest and use of library services and librarians. Lewis (2002) identified the following:

1. Those who work independently and rarely use the library services
2. Those who use the library frequently working with librarians and their research assistants
3. Those who use a combination of the two.

A three-tiered approach involving information, gathering, facilitating current awareness services and a librarian's proactive approach to support faculty member's needs make up Lewis' recommendations for the delivery of library services for faculty members.

Technology has further drawn faculty members away from library services so librarians have to work harder at engaging and collaborating with them. They are able to access electronic databases from anywhere, either at home or in their offices, and since many libraries have leaned towards electronic journals, they may no longer need the services of a librarian unless they are unable to find something. With this in mind, Lewis' three-tiered approach becomes highly relevant to academic law librarians.

The practice in many leading law school libraries is the liaison librarian services where a librarian is assigned to work with faculty members by assisting them with their library and information service needs. At the Osgoode Hall Law School Library the liaison librarian services was introduced in September 2006 and a librarian is assigned to a faculty member to assist them with their library research and information needs. This service was further extended to adjunct faculty in September 2009.

Graduate students (LL.M & Ph.D.)

This category of users engages in a considerable amount of research and so the library must provide adequate support to them especially since there is a timeline to their activities in the program. It is a common practice to find international students from around the world travelling to law schools in destinations like Canada, United Kingdom and the United States for post-graduate studies. One of the reasons for choosing the institutions is that there is a guarantee that they will have access to adequate library resources to support their research that may be lacking in their home countries. Similar to the liaison librarian service for faculty at the Osgoode Hall Law School Library, this service was also made available to graduate students in the full-time and research stream. Upon arrival, usually at the beginning of the academic year, liaison librarians meet on a one-on-one basis with graduate students to discuss their research areas and identify where they will need library support. Before the arrival of the students, with the support of the Graduate Programs Office, the library receives summaries of students' research proposals which are then distributed to librarians to review. Having access to these proposals gives librarians an insight into the research needs of the students and provides an opportunity for the library to plan what to add to its collection and learn what will be requested via interlibrary loans.

It is worthy mentioning that the following two subcategories exist among graduate students:

1. International graduate students whose first language is not English.
2. Graduate students who don't have a background in law. In other words, they don't have a first degree in law.
3. Graduate students coming from a different legal system. For example, some may be coming from civil legal systems to a common law system.

Librarians working in the law library may want to keep this important fact in mind when dealing with this subcategory. Those who fall into the second group will need a lot of help in understanding legal terminologies in the course of their work. It will be helpful if librarians can create research guides that will help this group of students. As for those coming from different legal systems, creating useful guides to help them understand the new environment will be extremely helpful.

Over the years this service has improved the profile of librarians in the Law School and as a result law librarians have been invited by graduate students to attend oral theses and dissertation presentations.

Undergraduate students (JD/LL.B)

The undergraduates/JD students are the main and active users of the library, especially the study space and the group study rooms where applicable. They spend most of their free time in-between classes in the library and use it as both a social and study space.

Distance education students

Distance learning students are usually enrolled in the undergraduate or graduate program for either a Masters or PhD. Some distance learning students are also enrolled in the part-time courses and some may be practitioners who are combining work with studies. These students may be enrolled in programmes where teaching takes place on satellite campuses or they may be located outside the city where the Law School is located. In these two instances there will be no librarian available to them, unlike other full-time students. The composition of the students in the distance learning stream is diverse and can be very challenging. Studies have shown that some of these students are mature students, some of whom are returning to school after a long break and are trying to adapt to a number of changes and developments in research, especially technology (Holloway, 2011). The library has an obligation to ensure that the necessary resources are made available to these students to support their research in order for them to complete the program. In a study of the research on library services for distance learning by academic libraries, Slade (2008) found that the emphasis has shifted from access to physical libraries and print materials to electronic libraries and electronic resources. Just like students in the full-time stream they will need to access readings to complete assignments and projects as well as write their research projects and dissertations. Before the advent of the Internet, services for distance education students were done mostly by sending materials to them in the mail or by fax. But the digital era has made things very easy and more reliable; they can access most of the materials at their convenience in their homes or other libraries closer to them. Many institutions have reciprocal borrowing agreements with other academic law libraries; part of this agreement may include conditions allowing distance learning students to borrow and use library materials from libraries closer to where they reside. Slade further noted that the growing number of remote users means that libraries need to develop services to support people accessing electronic resources from locations other than the campus libraries.

What are some of the major factors that the law library has to consider when designing and planning services for distance education students?

1. Identifying a contact (preferably a librarian) that the students can connect with whenever they have any library-related questions. This librarian will be responsible for organizing and facilitating orientation sessions for these users. Sessions will have to be conducted either over the telephone or over the Internet via video messaging. Hill et al (2013) in a survey of current practices in distance learning library services in urban and metropolitan universities in the United States found that two-thirds of libraries have a designated librarian or combination of specific librarians and staff members for facilitating services to this category of users. Their survey results also showed that the majority of the responsibility for distance learning students resided within the Reference Department. Ensuring that they are able to access library materials electronically is one of the critical factors as well as having a readily available contact for this group of users when they have questions or issues. The Osgoode Hall Law School facilitates a part-time LL.M program and some of its students are located in different parts of Canada as well as in international countries. The role of the law library is to ensure that these students have uninterrupted access to library resources and services. Library instruction is available to them at the same time as other students as it is shared through webcasts. The law library has invested in software through the IT department that can be used to provide one-on-one instruction to students, especially when teaching them how to work with electronic databases. Some of the students in this program are legal practitioners who are going back to school after a long time so they may need assistance with getting used to technology-based information.

2. Collection development decisions should be made to suit the needs of this category of users. For example, when acquiring electronic resources, academic law libraries that have these user groups should pay for multiple use of certain core materials so they may be used simultaneously.

3. Constant and continuous collaboration with Program Directors and Program Staff. Program Directors are the ones who design and manage courses in the distance learning program; the librarians should work with them to get information about new courses and work with them to facilitate library instruction and information literacy sessions.

Researchers

Most Law Schools have research centres and institutes affiliated to them. It is important for the library identify their needs and ensure that they acquire the necessary materials. The research focus varies so it means that the library will have materials and resources covering these disciplines. But with crunching budgets, this will be an advocacy role for the head of the library achieved by maintaining a good rapport with the heads of these centres. This may likely increase awareness that the library will need their financial support in order to sustain its collection for their needs. Since many of these centres receive external financial support, extending some support to the library collection budget may be considered.

Visiting fellows

These are academics, graduate students and legal practitioners who come to teach or research for a defined period. During their stay in the institution they place a very strong emphasis on accessing the library resources which may not be accessible to them in their home institutions. This group will need an introductory tour or orientation of the library because they are there for a short period. The library will usually plan for them to be given temporary library cards which will provide access to most of its resources for the period. Their privileges to certain services may be limited due to licensing agreements, budgetary or university policies.

Prospective students

Some may wonder why we need to include this category among the users of the law library since they are yet to gain admission to the institution. They are the potential candidates of the law school who need to know about library resources and facilities that will be available to them and which may assist them in making a decision to accept an offer or not. This means that the role of the library to these users is an advocacy and marketing one. Usually, at the Law School's Open House, the Law Librarian may be invited to make presentations about the library's resources and facilities for prospective students and their family members. This is an opportunity to showcase all of the valuable resources that will support their learning and research when they make a decision. The library's information is also usually included in the packages that are mailed out to them and displayed at career fairs. This means that it is highly critical and including prospective students when planning and designing library services and resources should not be overlooked.

Alumni

Members of the alumni often come back to use the law library collection since they already have an insight into the library collection. Upon graduation, most universities provide access to this group of users once they have registered as alumni. But there are restrictions and limited access to certain services and resources, especially electronic databases due to licensing agreements with service providers.

Members of the public

Some law libraries offer their services to members of the public, especially the publicly funded institutions. Self-representing litigants often value the availability and access to the resources and services of academic law libraries. However, with many library resources being available only electronically, this category of users may have limited access and have to rely on free legal websites. In this case, they may not need to come physically, but may seek the assistance of the Reference Librarian over the telephone or by email. Moreover, library spaces are often inadequate to accommodate additional users with the primary users so it is becoming increasingly difficult to provide services to this group of users.

Another group in this category will be law firm libraries requesting to use materials not available in their own collection; usually photocopying from print resources. They often send their staff to make photocopies or they may make a request through interlibrary loans, which is a revenue-generating service for the library.

Community colleges and private institutions around the library location also fall into this category. These institutions offer paralegal library technician, court administration and legal assistants courses but are unable to provide them with materials in a legal collection; the instructors often bring them to the nearest academic law libraries to show them some of the law reports and legislation collection. This has become problematic as many of these materials are now available electronically and it has become unnecessary to pay such visits. Access for these users will depend on each library's policy.

Users with disabilities

This category is spread across all the users that have been identified and could refer to faculty, students, alumni, visiting fellows or even members of the public. However, many libraries tend to leave the implementation of the policies for these users until the user walks through the door of the library. In defining disabilities, Mulliken and Lear (2013) observed that some disabilities such as physical and sensory ones are identifiable but learning, cognitive and some sensory ones are often not. They noted that there has been a shift from the legal definition of disabilities to the social model where the emphasis is more on the type of changes needed to accommodate disability. These are some of the questions and issues to be considered when planning and reviewing the library's policies:

- Is the library compliant with applicable legislation for providing access to users with disabilities?

  Many countries have legislation in place detailing the required and applicable guidelines for accessibility for users with disabilities. The United Nations' Convention on the Rights of Persons with Disabilities in Article 9(1) contains a list of requirements to be met by organizations in order to accommodate these users. Organizations are expected to remove 'obstacles and barriers to accessing information, communication and other services...' They are required to take appropriate measures to develop, promulgate and monitor the implementation of minimum standards and guidelines for the accessibility of facilities and services open or provided to the public among others.

- Is the library collection designed to accommodate these users?

  It is the duty of the library management to ensure that its resources and materials are easily accessible for these users. Where there is a visually impaired user, the library will ensure that this user has access to acceptable formats of the publications that will be required by them. Usually, the university asks these users to identify themselves so they can be provided with the required assistance. There are several software packages available for users with disabilities that interpret library resources. Database service providers provide audio recordings and web versions in their packages to support these users.

- Is the law library website compliant with the required policies and guidelines for users with disabilities?

  There are various requirements for the design, layout and display of websites to accommodate the needs of users with disabilities. Libraries must ensure that their website comply with these requirements such as the size of the font and the ability to modify these sizes by users with disabilities on their own, or the library's, equipment.

- Does the library provide support and services for users with disabilities when they come to use the library?

  It is important to ensure that access to library entrances is freely accessible by users in wheelchairs as well as having clearly marked buildings. In instances where the library entrance can only be accessed through a flight of stairs, there should be ramps for these users and nearby access to an elevator. Where the law library is on a multilevel facility it is critical to ensure that the elevator is working and made accessible for these users. The library representation should be clearly articulated when building renovations or audits are being carried out as this aspect is sometimes overlooked by other departments in the institution.

- Do you have a policy statement in place for users with disabilities?

  Having a clearly written policy guided by the institutional one on how the law library will service users with disabilities is a great asset. This document should be analyzed and reviewed periodically based on the services and the library's experience with these users. It should clearly state the steps and responsibilities of staff members when they encounter situations with this category of users. For example if a visually impaired student needs assistance with photocopying, staff at the information or circulation desk should be able to take immediate action, or if a user in a wheel chair needs to access the upper or lower floors of the library, they should be provided with access to the library elevators.

These are some of the critical questions that should be considered when preparing or updating the library's guidelines and policies for this category of users. Disabilities are sometimes usually generalized as physical, but following the institution's definition will be a starting point. It is important to note that while institutions tend to ask students and faculty to identify their disabilities; there are some individuals who are not comfortable with doing this. Some of them would rather approach the manager in charge to disclose their needs in a confidential manner and request assistance.

Mooting teams

For a clearer understanding of and exposure to the theories and practice of law, many law schools form mooting teams on different subject areas. Teams from different institutions compete amongst themselves and in some schools participating in these teams can be used to earn credits. Members of the mooting teams represent the law school at mooting competitions locally and internationally. They work on different subject areas; this requires rigorous and intensive coaching ahead of the competitions. They will often make requests for library materials that may not necessarily be acquired by the library in which case they still have to be accommodated. Some law libraries also assign study carrels for mooting teams inside the library as well as after-hours access. Special privileges are also created in the library's circulation policies to accommodate their loans.

Law journal editors

Many law schools, especially in North America, have student-managed publications in addition to faculty-managed ones. These publications are supervised by faculty members. In the case of faculty publications, they use the services of students to review and edit the submissions for publication. These students often require the assistance of the Reference Librarian with citation checks for cases, articles and legislation. They make use of the library extensively all year round.

Conclusion

Having identified some of the user categories that exist in an academic law library setting, how does the library ensure that they are reaching out to these users? Thompson (2012) noted that the challenge for libraries is to promote effective use and full exploitation of electronic resources as well as the physical space and print collections by marketing and proactive measures. Library users are the consumers of the services and products being made available to them, hence the need to make the library visible by branding these resources and building a relationship with these users. Branding the library can be done by displaying and announcing the strengths, unique and successful products and services available in the library. Build a library blog, coordinate who will write and post on a weekly or daily basis. Social media is a great tool for marketing library services but it must be professionally utilized. Create a virtual tour of the library so the prospective student has a visual idea of what the library space looks like. Make this look appealing even if library renovations are being planned.

This chapter has identified the users of the academic law library and their potential needs. It is critical and mandatory that the librarians managing and working in the academic library should understand the types of users they will be dealing with. A proactive approach to understanding the users of the library will help in building and maintaining the library's relevance in the law school.

Collection development/ management $\boxed{3}$

The law library collection

The academic law library collection is distinctly unique but very expensive to manage and update. Unique in the sense that some the materials being used in the law school library are the ones the law students continue to use when they graduate and start working as practitioners. Law reports and statute books are common tools that are used by legal practitioners as they need to cite precedents from these materials in order to be successful in their career.

Materials found in academic law libraries

It is important for any librarian working in the law library to understand the nature of the collection. A librarian should be able to identify and know how to work with these materials. Reference librarians will be required to show students how to work with different materials. Technical service librarians will be interested in being able to identify the materials whether they are responsible for ordering or cataloguing; they should be able to distinguish between a book, journal, law report or an electronic resource. Law materials come in both print and electronic formats; but lately there has been a drastic impact through technological advancements as many resources are now available electronically. Many academic law libraries have replacing them with a large number of their print subscriptions, mostly journals and law reports online versions. Users of the academic law library will be interested in using the identified materials for their research. Because the law is constantly changing and new legislation is being passed all the time, academic law libraries need to regularly update their collection. Smith (2010) noted that the law is an integral part of a constantly evolving social landscape and a study of the law promotes accuracy of expression. Legal researchers constantly want to keep abreast of any new developments in their research areas so it is important to always keep track of any newly published materials especially in newer subject areas.

Legal materials are classified as Primary and Secondary sources in most Common Law countries.

Primary sources are very important in the collection of every academic law library. They constitute the persuasive and binding authority of lawmakers and the court. Cohen and Olson (2013) describe primary resources as the official pronouncements of governments and lawmakers that form the basis of the legal doctrine. In the legal profession there is a lot of emphasis and reliance on judicial precedents and statute law or the principle of *stare decisis*. This is a standard skill-set of a lawyer; the ability to be able to persuade the court with other cases in order to win an argument. New statutes and regulations are being written and modified all the time; they will be referred to by the courts and applied by government to the citizens.

Primary sources

Primary sources contain the actual statement of the law. They are the original work of lawmakers and members of the judiciary. They can be found in bills, statutes, regulations, law reports, constitutions and treaties.

Law reports − Law reports contain decisions and judgments of the courts, with some published by the courts and others available through commercial publishers. In some jurisdictions there are official publishers of law reports. One example is the Supreme Court of Canada which publishes its judgments in the Supreme Court Law Reports. Note that this law report contains only cases that are heard in the Supreme Court of Canada. Other commercial law reports such as the Dominion Law Report will also carry reports of the Supreme Court of Canada in their publication with permission. There is also the All England Law Reports which are published by a commercial publisher. This law report contains cases heard in different levels of courts in United Kingdom from the House of Lords to the high courts. In the United States, West Publishing is the leading publisher of case reporters and is organized by geographical location.

Matters heard before administrative tribunals are also available in print through commercial publishers or published by the tribunals. In the digital age, many of these decisions are available on their websites. Selected courts and administrative tribunal decisions for some jurisdictions are available on Legal Information Institutes (LIIs) such as AustLII, BaiLII, CanLII, SafLII among others.

Unreported judgments or cases − It is important to understand that not all cases that are heard in courts are reported or published in law reports; these cases are referred to as unreported judgments. This means that cases that fall under this category will not be found in any law report. In some jurisdictions law reporters will only publish the cases that are heard by the highest court of the jurisdiction. These unreported judgments can only be accessed by being requested directly from the court houses. LexisNexis Quicklaw carries a lot of unreported decisions from Canadian provincial courts in its database. The LIIs such as AustLII, BaiLII and CanLII all make available unreported judgments from some jurisdictions. And in Nigeria the practice is for law reports to publish cases heard before the highest courts: the Supreme Court of Nigeria and the Federal Court of Appeal, and not those of the lower courts.

Legislation − Legislation is made for the citizens by publicly elected officers. They include statutes, regulations and legislative materials. Statutes are laws that are made through the law-making process which differ in every jurisdiction. Regulations are subordinate legislation that provide the details of how a statute is enforced by the government.

Legislative materials include bills, debates, committee reports and journals.

Bills are part of the law-making process and they include all the details of how a law came into existence. They include all the discussions that took place among law-makers before they agreed to write the law. In some instances where a bill does not become law, the bill gives the history of why this happened and it then becomes a reference for the future. The bill-making process varies in each jurisdiction which means that the number of pages and the format may vary.

Debates are published transcription of conversations that take place in the legislature of different countries. These debates give the details of what each law-maker said in the law-making process.

Committee reports and journals provide details of questions that are asked by law-makers in the law-making process. They help citizens understand the reasons why a law was promulgated in the first place; these reports and journals describe the activities of the law-makers who reviewed the law and drafted it.

Treaties – Treaties are documents that contain agreements that are signed between countries. They constitute binding agreements between nation states on mutually agreed upon interests such as trade, immigration, employment among others.

Gazettes & Government Documents – These are government publications containing announcements about government activities including the promulgation of legislation. For example, in Canada, Part II of the Canada Gazette contains Regulations while Part III contains the Acts of Parliament. In smaller jurisdictions in Africa, South America and the Caribbean available government documents are limited to government gazettes, Hansards and committee reports. Most government documents for the United Kingdom, United States, Canada and the European countries are now mostly available in electronic format.

Case law and legislation are available through different sources. They are available through the courts, government printers and commercial publishers. In many jurisdictions especially Australia, Canada, United Kingdom and the United States legislation is made available electronically on government websites; the turnaround time for making new laws available is usually very fast, ranging from two business days to one month. The Legal Information Institutes (LIIs) of the world also make legislation and case law freely available on the Internet. The government sites and legal information institutes provide access to primary resources dating from the early and late 1990s to the present. One of the developments in legal publishing is for commercial publishers and academic institutions to make available in digital format historical and early law reports and legislation. For example, HeinOnline provides access to digitized historical legislation and legislative materials for the United States. Also, LLMC Digital has digitized several volumes of historical legislation and case law from the United States, Canada, United Kingdom and Commonwealth countries such as Nigeria, Kenya and selected countries in the English-speaking Caribbean.

The following is a list of government websites that provide access to primary resources:

Canada
Legislation
Federal justice - http://laws.justice.gc.ca/

This is the website of the federal government of Canada and it provides access to federal laws. It is available in English and French. Each province has its own website and they are linked to the Canadian Legal Information Institute (CanLII).
Bills & Debates - http://laws-lois.justice.gc.ca/
This is the website of the Parliament of Canada and it provides access to bills and debates before the Senate of Canada and the House of Commons.
United Kingdom
Legislation — http://www.legislation.gov.uk
This website carries the official statutes for the United Kingdom, Scotland, Wales and Northern Ireland.
Bills — http://www.parliament.co.uk
This website provides access to bills that are before the Parliament with an archive of the earlier ones.
United States
Legislation & Bills - https://beta.congress.gov/
This is the website of the United States Congress with access to legislation, congressional record and committee proceedings.

Legal Information Institutes (LIIs) — The Legal Information Institutes is a collaborative project that provides free access to legal information on the Internet. It covers about 123 jurisdictions and I have chosen to discuss the selected ones below:

Australian Legal Information Institute (AustLII) — This database provides access to legal information of Australia, including secondary sources.

Asian Legal Information Institute (AsianLII) — AsianLII covers 28 Asian countries providing access to legislation, case law, law reform reports and law journals.

British and Irish Legal Information Institute (BaiLII) — BaiLII contains case law, legislation, books and law commission reports for the United Kingdom, England & Wales, Scotland, Northern Ireland, Jersey, Ireland, Court of Justice of the European and the European Court of Human Rights. This database uniquely highlights leading case law by subject.

Canadian Legal Information Institute (CanLII) — CanLII provides access to legislation and case law from the Supreme Court of Canada, Federal courts, provincial courts and administrative tribunals. It features noting up tools that can help researchers find the latest updates to legislation as well as offering tools that identify cases that have cited sections of a legislation and legislation that is cited in cases.

Commonwealth Legal Information Institute (CommonLII) — This database provides access to case law and legislation from 60 Commonwealth and common law countries. CommonLII also includes access to the English Reports 1220—1873. Many of the Commonwealth countries are developing countries where law reporting and publication of legislation is very inconsistent therefore making it difficult to access; but the collaborative efforts of the legal information institutes has assisted in creating free access to them.

South African Legal Information Institute (SAFLII) — SAFLII provides access to case law, legislation and secondary resources from 16 southern and eastern African countries. This includes materials from regional institutions like the East African Court of Justice.

Cornell Legal Information Institute (CornellLII) − CornellLII provides access to United States Code, Supreme Court decisions, Code of Federal Regulations and other state legal materials. One of its unique features is the Wex legal dictionary and encyclopedia.

Legal Information Institute of India (LIIofIndia) − This is one of the newer additions to the legal information movement. It provides access to the Indian Code, state legislation, case law from the Supreme Court, High Courts and tribunals, treaties and journals. LIIofIndia features LawCite, a tool which shows the citation history of cases, legislation and articles.

World Legal Information Institute (WorldLII) − WorldLII provides a single search engine for legal information from AustLII, BaiLII, CanLII, HKLII, Cornell LII and PacLII.

Many law libraries rely on these websites because of the extensive coverage especially for foreign jurisdictions and so you will find that some academic law libraries have cancelled some of their major subscriptions as a result of this development.

Secondary sources

Secondary sources contain the opinion of specialists and experts in various areas of the law. Secondary sources provide current and up-to-date information about cases and legislation; they are usually the first step in legal research as they help the researcher to understand the legal issue. A legal encyclopedia, for example, provides a broader definition and explanation of an issue by pointing and referring the reader to available legislation, case law and books. These sources are simply explanations of the law and are often cited in courts, especially if their authors are considered leading authorities in that subject area. Secondary sources are therefore considered as persuasive authority since they can influence the decisions of judges. Examples of secondary sources include:

Textbooks and treatises − They are usually written by leading authorities in the subject matter who could be academics, legal practitioners and judges. Note that there are student textbooks and practitioners' texts. In many cases students' textbooks are easily worded explaining the principles of law citing legislation and case law; whereas practitioners' books are for legal practitioners and explain the theories and forms of practice. Depending on the library's budget, practitioners' texts may not necessarily be acquired by academic law libraries unless some titles are explicitly requested by faculty or the accreditation requirements. Textbooks come in bound or loose-leaf formats.

Law journals − They are published by law schools, bar associations and commercial legal publishers. Law journals are an invaluable component of an academic law library. The content of the articles published in law journals cover most of the current issues and ongoing debates in law. Cohen and Olson (2013) described academic legal journals as a major forum where legal academics debate and develop theories. The content of a law journal includes articles, commentaries on current leading cases and book reviews. Many leading law schools in the world publish at least one law journal named after their institution. Law journals are different from journals from other disciplines because they are usually published by law schools and edited by the students with faculty advisers. Student editors gather a lot of research experience while working in these roles and also build their research skills.

The latest trend in the digital age is for some law journals to be made available only electronically, especially on open access initiative websites. Examples of these journals include − Web Journal of Current Legal Issues (http://webjcli.org/) and the German Law Journal (http://www.germanlawjournal.com/). HeinOnline provides the largest online access to digitized journals and law reviews dating back to the 19th century.

Legal Periodical Indexes − Indexes help legal researchers to efficiently locate journal articles. Some of the indexes contain abstracts while others provide full text access to the articles. Examples of legal periodical indexes include LegalTrac, Legal Source formerly called Index to Legal Periodicals, Index to Foreign Legal Periodicals, and Index to Canadian Legal Periodicals.

Legal encyclopedias − Legal encyclopedias provide extensive and detailed explanations of the theories and issues of law using references on how they have been applied in case law, legislation, articles and textbooks. They are usually published as multiple volume series and are updated with new areas and topics of law. Each volume covers different subjects of law and the authors are leading experts in these areas. The most common series of legal encyclopedia published in many Commonwealth countries is the Halsburys Laws series; there are the Halsburys Laws of England, Halsburys Laws of Australia, Halsburys Laws of Singapore, Halsburys Laws of Nigeria and the most recent is the Halsburys Laws of Canada.

Other examples of legal encyclopedias are the American Jurisprudence which focuses on the law of the United States and the Canadian Encyclopedic Digest.

There are also practice encyclopedias which contain forms and precedents that are used by legal practitioners but may be needed in academic law libraries. Examples of these include the Encyclopedia of Forms and Precedents and O'Brien's Encyclopedia of Forms and Precedents. These volumes contain samples and templates of forms that are used by legal practitioners such as contract forms and court forms.

Law dictionaries − Legal terminologies are different and can be complex as some of the words originate from the Roman and Latin languages. Law dictionaries provide the definition, meaning and translations of these terminologies.

Examples of law dictionaries include the following:

1. Black's Law Dictionary − This dictionary predominantly covers legal terminologies of the United States.
2. Osborne's concise law dictionary (the first edition is available for free on the Internet archives - https://archive.org/details/conciselawdictio030371mbp) − It covers legal terminologies from the United Kingdom and Commonwealth countries.
3. Stroud's Judicial Dictionary of Words and Phrases − This is a practitioner's dictionary but is used in academic law libraries as well. It covers the terminologies of the United Kingdom and Commonwealth countries.
4. The Dictionary of Canadian Law − It covers the legal terminologies for Canada
5. The Nigerian Law Dictionary − It covers the legal terminologies for Nigeria.

Theses and dissertations — These are the academic publications of post-graduate submitted to the institution as part of the requirements to fulfil the completion of advanced degrees. They constitute a fundamental resource for students in the graduate program. Depending on the library policy they are usually bound volumes found in a separate area of the collection or in the institutional repository. More recently theses and dissertations are being digitized by individual institutions and are available electronically; some institutions have partnered with Proquest who make it available as part of a database.

Audiovisual resources — These resources come in the form of microfiche, microform, videos, CDs, DVDs. Legal fiction is available on DVDs and they are very popular and heavily used in many academic law libraries. A lot of historical legal materials are available in microform and microfiche. Videos and CDs have become obsolete with more emphasis on DVDs, talking books, online streaming etc.

Special Collections — The materials designated as Special Collections in most academic law libraries include older materials originally published from the jurisdiction where the library is located that are over 100 years old, faculty publications, casebooks, manuscripts, reports and festschrifts. Each library has its own policy for materials to be found in this area of the library. Depending on the size of the library, Special Collections materials are stored in a room inside the library or in a special part of the library and there are restrictions and special policies for user access.

Past Exams — Students often want to consult past examination question papers. The law library will usually coordinate with the Student Services Department of the School to make them available. The latest trend is to digitize them and make them available through the student's portal on the Law School's website.

Loose-leaf materials

Because of the changing nature of the law, some publications have to be updated periodically as soon as new information is available or changes are made to the law. Loose-leaf materials are issued as updates to whole works, this requires that the new information is added and the old one is discarded. The rising costs of these materials have seen them gradually being phased out in academic law libraries as subscriptions to many of these titles are being discontinued.

The traditional format of primary and secondary legal resources was originally print; however with technological advancements, the legal publishing industry has introduced significant transformation with the introduction of new formats. Electronic books are very common among legal publishers such as Oxford, Cambridge, Irwin Law Books, LexisNexis Butterworths, Thomson Reuters, HeinOnline among others. The academic law librarian must understand the trends in legal publishing in order to be able to recommend and acquire materials in the collection.

The academic law library collection is defined by the following:

1. Library Budget — The size and amount of the library budget plays a highly significant role in defining the size of its collection. The amount of money that is available in the budget will be the yardstick for measuring how much will be spent on collections. In a centralized system the law library is treated as a branch library and will get the same amount as the

other libraries in the system. Depending on the administrative structure, the law library may not necessarily receive more funding even though materials are known to be very expensive and highly priced. In an autonomous administrative system there will be direct input and control from the Law School on the law library's budget. This will also depend on the level of support given to the library by the Law School's administration. Some Law Schools have been fortunate to have library-centric, proactive and supportive Deans who always fund the law library from any fundraising initiative they have embarked on. However, the bottom line is that the more funding that the library has at its disposal, the more it is able to spend on acquiring materials for its collection. Academic law libraries worldwide have been severely impacted by declining economies and this has resulted in library closures and assimilation of law collection with the main library collection.

2. Courses offered in the Law Program – Law Schools tend to have different subject focus depending on the specialization or areas of research of their professors and research, which means that they don't have the same course offerings. However, note that there are some compulsory courses which are taught in universally all schools such as Constitutional, Criminal, and Legal Writing and Research Some law schools may have faculty with research interests in International Law, Employment and Labour Law, Legal History, Intellectual Property and Corporate Law. As a result, the course offerings may be centred on these subject areas. This implies that the library collection must be very strong in these areas. If the law school is offering graduate programs, steps must be taken to ensure that the collection is able to support the needs of students in this program.

3. Requirements of Accrediting Bodies – As discussed in chapter one, accrediting bodies have a strong role to play in the existence of law programmes all over the world. One of the standards and a requirement of the accreditation bodies is that academic law libraries should have specific materials in their collection. These standards vary in each jurisdiction; in some instances, these organizations provide lists of required materials that they expect to find in these libraries. Academic law libraries in the United States and Nigeria continue to ensure that their libraries meet these standards.

4. Number of Students – The number of students in a program plays a critical role in determining the number of copies that the library will acquire for its collection. These numbers have a strong influence on decisions when signing contracts for electronic access for multiple users or multiple copies of heavily-used and core materials.

Managing academic library collections

Collection development is the building and managing of the library's collection in print and electronic format. Technological advancements have seen the transition of many law resources in electronic and digital formats. Gregory (2011) observed that: "The fast-growing user preference for electronic resources has severely impacted the collection development budgets of most libraries. Because the new electronic library resources usually do not completely supplant existing materials, purchasing them does not eliminate the cost of buying print formats." The trend is shifting towards having an electronic law library collection can be attributed to the following reasons:

1. Shrinking library budgets   The financial climate continues to impact organizational budgets and this does not leave out libraries in academic institutions, law firms, judiciaries

and other types of law libraries. In addition to shrinking library budgets, academic libraries have been faced with high exchange and inflation rates as many materials are acquired from overseas. As a result many law library directors or administrators have been forced to weigh their options when making collection development decisions.

2. Reductions of library space − Many law libraries have experienced space reduction which has mostly resulted in the loss of shelf space. In some academic law libraries where the library is situated in the law school building, library space has been taken over to accommodate the law school's needs. While in law firms, the cost of real property has forced many organizations to reduce library space to accommodate their financial constraints. In either of these situations, the introduction of electronic and digital formats is a supportive alternative method of providing library resources to users. However, in the academic library where library space is still a necessity, it has continued to be a major challenge when the library is unable to provide adequate study space for its users. However, some may argue that library space may be irrelevant as many of the library collection are now available electronically and as a result users may not need to physically go to the library.

3. Trends in legal publishing − As mentioned earlier in this chapter, a lot has changed in the legal publishing industry in the last decade with technological advancements. A librarian managing a law library collection should have a sound knowledge of and high level of familiarity with trends in legal publishing. A strong business acumen combined with negotiating skills will be helpful and useful during the collection, development and management process. Legal publishing over the years has seen a lot of technological improvements such as the extinction of formats like the CD-ROM and the introduction of online and digital space with perpetual ownership. The advent of the Internet paved the way for information being freely available, legal materials can be accessed anywhere and anytime. Legal publishers have continued to digitize legal materials by giving varying options to academic law libraries. The trend now is for academic law libraries to rely more on electronic information. Bernstein and Canaan (2013) have concluded that as more information is provided electronically, the day of the print collection is fast becoming a thing of the past. With changes in world of legal publishing, academic law libraries are left with no other choice but to adapt to these developments. Many law reports, law journals and statute books have been digitized which means that academic law library directors have no other option than to subscribe to them. Then there are the legal information institutes that are making this information available on the Internet for free. An example of this is the Canadian Legal Information Institute (CanLII) funded by practicing lawyers in Canada. CanLII provides access to Canadian cases and legislation from the Federal, provincial and territorial governments. The availability of these resources even though they do not carry historical information will help supplement access to legal information in the era where libraries are facing significant budgetary cuts and space challenges.

A librarian working in academic law libraries needs a clear understanding and knowledge of all the issues that may impact the management of the library's collection. Law Schools tend to create and introduce additional programs and courses. The librarian needs to plan the library budget accordingly to accommodate these demands.

Law library collection development policy

A collection development policy is a document that defines and describes what the library acquires in its collection. This document will identify the library's objectives in building its collections to support the law school's academic objectives. Having a collection development policy is a professional way of building and managing the library's collection. According to Gregory (2011) the purposes of a collection development policy are to inform and direct library processes in acquiring and making resources available to users as well as serving as a protection for the library against challenges to its procedures and resources. This means that the collection development policy protects the library from challenges arising from complaints of library users about the library collection. Pickett et al (2011) described collection development policies as an effective communication tool and a document that helps libraries demonstrate accountability to its stakeholders. Garavaglia (2013) defined the collection development policy as a blueprint or architectural drawing needed to build the collection. In the United States the ABA accreditation standard Section 606–6 requires that law school libraries should create and formulate collection development policies for their collection.

The collection development policy should be written by the head of the library after due consultation with librarians and library staff. The input of faculty members who may be members of the Library Committee may be very relevant when preparing the document. It is critical and important to have the input of librarians and library staff as they are the ones dealing directly with library users and will have an idea of the usage of library materials. For example, reference librarians will know how often they refer students or faculty to some databases, circulation staff will have an idea of how often particular books were charged out as well as the number of holds and be able to recall the demand for certain titles by users at the Circulation Desk. Technical services librarians and staff will be able to add their input on the usage statistics of databases received from vendors and service providers. Faculty input is important because they will be able to lend their voice at management meetings or when necessary to justify why the law library budget must be consistently increased every financial year.

A good collection development policy will help define the scope and breadth of materials and resources available in the library. This policy will be drafted with the specializations and needs of its users in mind. In other words, acquisition of materials will be made to support the law school's curriculum and the research focus of the faculty. For example, in an academic or research law library, the collection development policy will feature the research areas of the law school professors, its graduate and undergraduate students and research centres that are affiliated with the law school. In the law firm, the collection development policy will focus on the practice areas and specializations of the practitioners. Collection development policies should be updated periodically and as needed; they should not be personalized to the likes and dislikes of library administrators. For example, a typical collection development policy should include the continuous acquisition of the primary resources for the jurisdiction such as law reports and statutes. Or the compulsory acquisition of materials published by law professors in that institution in the case of an academic law library.

Suggested guidelines that can be considered when writing a collection development policy for an academic law library:

- Identify your users – This involves the library director and the librarians identifying the primary users of the library collection and the purpose. For example, in an academic library, the practice is to identify faculty, undergraduate, post-graduate and researchers as the primary users of the collection. This section of the policy may also need to identify and highlight the strong areas of research in that institution. In some law schools there may be more focus on taxation and constitutional or corporate law by the faculty, in which case the collection will be very strong in those areas.

- Identify the format of materials to be acquired — This part of the policy may address decisions on the type of format that the library will acquire whether it is in print or in electronic. This decision is usually determined by the amount of funding available in the library's budget, the availability of library space and the price of the resources. Given the trend in legal publishing with digitized periodicals such as journals, law reports and statutes; many academic law libraries are opting for electronic versions rather than print.
- Assign collection development responsibilities to librarians — In large academic law libraries, where you have about 4 or 5 professional librarians the practice is to assign subject areas for them to maintain. They will work under the guidance and consultation of the library director who gives approval and signs off on their recommendations. These librarians sometimes work with faculty members when they are making selections in their subject areas so as to get a specialist opinion. However, in smaller law libraries, collection development tasks will be the sole responsibility of the Manager/Librarian.
- Make policies on the number of copies — It is a good practice to have a written policy on the number of copies to be purchased when buying print materials. Again, this is determined by the size of the library's budget, the number of users and space available for library growth. This will include policies on the number of copies the library will be acquiring for course readings.
- Identify a policy on gifts, replacements and weeding — It is always helpful to have a clearly written policy on the library's practice of gifts and donations. It is a common practice for libraries to receive donations of all kinds from different donors, especially estates of legal practitioners or retired legal practitioners; but clearly not all the materials will be useful to the library. A common practice is to have the donor send an itemized list with the titles that they wish to donate. A library may decide to accept some titles that are not available at all in its collection or it may decide to replace stolen or damaged copies of certain titles but usually it is best to see the list and identify what is useful and relevant. Librarians should learn to turn down donations and gifts to their collections. In this section of the policy, it may be helpful to identify when library titles that are damaged or missing from the collection should be replaced. For example, if certain pages are missing from the 1st edition of a required title in the reading list; should the library look to buying the 1st edition from a used book seller or buy the latest edition of this title? This part of the policy should also state when the library will weed out its collection. Weeding as a library activity is discussed in a latter part of this book. This will include statements on whether the newer editions of textbooks will be moved from the Reserve collection to the General collection.
- Identify a policy on Special Collections and Rare Books — Many law libraries have designated materials that are categorized as "special collections and rare books" but this definition varies in different countries. A part of the collection development policy forms a great place to define and identify the components of this section of the library's collection.
- Make a policy on when the collection development document will be updated. It is important to identify how often the document will be revised even though there should be a level of flexibility as new situations arise all the time.

- Identify cooperative agreements with other institutions. Academic law libraries usually have mutual agreements with law libraries to loan each other materials from their collections. These agreements usually ensure that the loan period for the materials borrowed is implemented by the lending library.

Pickett et al noted that many libraries do not commit the time and labour required to write collection development policies, nor review and update them. While sharing their experience about the revival of the collection development policy statement at Texas A&M University, they suggested that long-term planning that targets the promotion and management of this tool will evolve with the organization and not become an optional activity. It is important that the collection development policy should be reviewed and modified periodically to regularly adapt to changing circumstances, according to Knudsen (2011).

Collection development policy documents for most academic law libraries in the United States, Canada and the United Kingdom are available on their websites. Law libraries in the following leading law schools have made their collection development policies available on the Internet:

United States
1. Lilian Goldman Law Library, Yale University
2. Harvard Law School Library
3. Goodson Law Library, Duke University Law School
4. University of Michigan-Ann Arbor Law Library
5. Cornell University Law Library
6. Edward Bennett Williams Law Library, Georgetown University
7. Kresge Law Library, University of Notre Dame
8. Washington University Law School Library

United Kingdom
1. King's College London
2. Squire Law Library, Cambridge University
3. Bodleian Law Library, Oxford University

Canada
1. Nahum Gelber Law Library, McGill University
2. Osgoode Hall Law School, York University
3. William R. Lederman Law Library, Queen's University
4. John & Dotsa Bitove Family Law Library, Western University (formerly University of Western Ontario)

Selection process

The selection of library materials is the joint responsibility of the head of the library and the librarians in the team. The recommendations received from faculty members, students - especially graduates - and researchers also play a critical role in the selection process. Depending on the size of the library and the number of professional librarians that are available, each librarian may be assigned different subject areas in the library's collection to manage. This task involves updating all print or electronic resources by ensuring that the library's collection is current and meets the needs of its users. Another deciding factor in selecting library resources, especially in print format, is to weigh the purchase cost of the material against the cost of requesting that material through inter-library loans. The librarian may present their recommendation to the library director who can either approve or disapprove it.

It is a common practice for law libraries to post a suggestion for purchase form on their website where recommendations may be submitted electronically. These requests automatically go to a designated staff member who reviews and follows the appropriate library policy before a decision is made on whether or not to purchase the material.

Selecting electronic resources

As noted earlier in this chapter, the shifting trend in many academic law libraries' acquisition practices from print to electronic resources is due to developments in legal publishing and emerging technologies. One of the drawbacks of this trend is that in fiscal and accounting terms electronic resources are classified as expenses while print materials i.e. books are considered as capital. Nonetheless, many academic law libraries are adopting this option as they are facing a lot of financial cuts and there is a constant demand for library space. Many institutions that have collection development policies have revised them to reflect this trend. It is important that librarians demonstrate some critical skills when selecting electronic resources. Vendors are marketers and tend to present attractive bundles with short term cost savings. The librarian, before making decisions, must weigh the pros and cons of each product. The following factors should be considered when making decisions about electronic resources:

- Cost — Before making a decision about acquiring electronic it is always best to analyze the cost implication to the library's budget by considering a number of issues. For example, if a book is available in print and also as an eBook; what will be the cost benefits to buying the eBook rather than the print and what are the conditions placed in the contract for this purchase? Alternatively, if it's a law report that the publisher is now only making available electronically at an astronomical and unreasonable price, will it eat into the library's budget? Some of the things to consider in this situation will be whether or not the cases can be found elsewhere either on free or government websites. Another consideration is whether or not a subject-specific law report is a main focus of researchers in the law school. The librarian should factor in all these issues before making a decision.
- Read available reviews from other institutions — Reviews are now available on popular legal blogs where law librarians share their views and opinions about new resources. Librarians as information providers don't hesitate to share their experiences through these media. They have proved to be very useful and invaluable to some of us! Some librarians have also used listservs to gather opinions and suggestions about new electronic resources; such answers have been collated and posted for the use of others.

- Contact other professionals — Asking for other people's opinion is never a bad idea, especially if it's going could to save you from making a big mistake. If this is a new product, ask what other libraries are going to purchase and their reasons; compare notes with them if your user types are similar. This can assist a great deal with decision-making.
- Gather the opinion of in-house team — If your library is a big one with more than two professional librarians in your team; it will be helpful to gather the opinion of other members of the team, get everyone to review the product. The members of your team can involve the faculty members they work with and get their opinions about the product. There are also listservs for different groups through the various professional associations where opinions can be gathered.
- Always ask for a trial and demo — Many vendors provide a trial for their new products; some also offer demonstration sessions. Creating time for a demo with members of your team allows you to ask questions and get more information from the vendor. Participating in some of these sessions has helped me to identify some potential issues that I would not have picked up otherwise.

Selection tools

Librarians use different methods to receive information about new publications from publishers. The following are examples of selection methods that are used in academic law libraries:

- Publisher's website and social media tools — Publishers use technology as a marketing tool to reach out to their stakeholders by posting information about their latest publications on their website. It is a common practice to set up email alerts to receive announcements about new publications. And lately they send out tweets or post messages on other social media sites. One of the advantages of using publisher's websites is that information is received instantly, unlike when catalogs and brochures have to be mailed out and sometimes get lost or take longer to reach their intended destination.
- Book Jobbers and Specialist Booksellers — The practice in many academic law libraries is to outsource the supply of books and serials to book jobbers and specialist booksellers. This entails the library contracting out the supply of law materials to the book jobber; part of the responsibilities in the agreement is that the book jobber will ensure that the library receives all the latest editions of titles in its collection as well as other relevant publications as they become available. Each library has its own terms and agreements; some book jobbers may supply only books and not periodicals. These suppliers also classify, catalogue, label and process the materials making them shelf-ready by the time they arrive in the library. Many academic law libraries in these hard financial times are using this option as it saves them a lot of money. The use of book jobbers for legal acquisitions has worked very well in academic law libraries with a centralized system as many of them have either phased out their Technical Services Department or this department never existed in the first place. Examples of the book jobbers are Yankee Book Peddler Inc. (YBP), HeinOnline and Gaunt Inc, Books in print, Coutts.

  Specialist booksellers are often contracted to supply materials for the library's Special Collection and Rare Books. It is a common practice for them to supply manuscripts, letters, festschrifts or any rare legal materials.

- Using specialist booksellers - Examples of specialist booksellers include Wildy and Sons Ltd, Law Book Exchange and Meyer Boswell Books Inc. Using specialist booksellers ensures that the library buys the right material and it saves a lot of time for libraries where there is no Special Collection and Rare Books librarian.

Acquisitions

This is the process of ordering and buying books, serials and electronic resources. Acquisitions are carried out by any of the following methods:

1. Direct purchase of materials from publishers — The Acquisitions department can make a purchase directly from publishers, booksellers and online services such as Amazon. These purchases are made as the need arises.
2. By subscription, standing orders or approval plans — This is the most popular method of acquiring library materials. The Acquisition department sets up subscription, standing orders and approval plans for serials and books. As the majority of legal materials are published on a periodical basis, the library sets up these services in order to receive the latest publications. Approval plans are set up with book jobbers like YBP, HeinOnline and Coutts to receive publications as and when they are available based on a defined budget.

The Acquisitions department is responsible for the managing of invoices, payment of bills, and coordinating and processing materials when received. These activities are carried out by recording invoices in the integrated library system or by using other external databases. Some libraries still use a manual system using slips received from vendors. Examples of electronic acquisitions can be found in library systems such as SIRSI and VOYAGER. The electronic system allows a coordination and inventory of library materials; all the records are linked together for cataloguing, circulation and library catalogue. Users from the library catalogue are able to trace the history of print materials that are available in the library collection. For those using the manual system, the records are filed away in filing cabinets; a major disadvantage of this is that the records are prone to disasters such as floods and fires or can be misplaced.

The Acquisitions department is usually in the Technical Services area in many academic law libraries. Acquisitions involve some basic bookkeeping skills to ensure that the library's account is coordinated as well as having a great sense of organization. This area of the library ensures that books and periodicals on standing order are received on time; in addition, this area is responsible for monitoring financial records to make sure that publishers and book vendors are paid as and when necessary.

Weeding

The library's collection development policy will include a section on the library's weeding activities. Weeding a library's collection involves removing materials that are out of date with newer editions or damaged materials from the shelves. Each library will have its own weeding criteria, involving steps and roles for staff in different areas. For example, it is the duty of the Circulation staff to remove weeded materials from the shelves and then pass it on to Technical Services cataloging staff who will update the records in the integrated library system or relocate the material to another part of the collection. In an academic law library, weeding is done during the quiet period when students are on holidays and when there is less traffic on the shelves. Usually, librarians will be assigned different areas in the collection to weed; this involves taking a look at the books available and ensuring that the library has current editions of each title. In a library with an extensive collection, some of the older materials may not necessarily be discarded and thrown out of the collection; they may be moved to other areas of the library such as the Special Collections. Weeding may also be necessary where a library is downsizing its collection and it's necessary to create more study space for users. This seems to be a trend in some academic libraries in which case electronic materials are being substituted for print. For example, some libraries are no longer collecting print versions of United States law reports and statutes since they are freely available online or through commercial vendors. Another example is discontinuing statutes and law reports that are available through the Legal Information Institutes like CanLII, AustLII etc. This step frees a lot of library space and allows each library to utilize space and resources as they want. As is expected, librarians will need to carry out a lot of weeding in order to come to such decisions.

Copyright & licensing

Information technology has changed the way we access library materials and this has impacted policies and procedures. Since the majority of resources are now in electronic format and are born digital, libraries must pay a great deal of attention to copyright and licensing agreements that are to be signed with publishers and vendors. Depending on the size of the library and administrative arrangements, the law library and the main library usually have a joint responsibility in managing copyright agreements for some electronic resources. It has become a common practice to have a librarian who is in charge of managing all digital and electronic resources, is responsible for all copyright and licensing documents and liaises with the head of the library.

Inter-library loans

The inter-library loans service allows the borrowing and lending of library materials between related institutions. Each library sets its own policy for the operation of this service. Many libraries don't allow their materials to travel too far but it is a very useful cost-saving alternative that has provided researchers with access to the gaps in the collection of their home institutions. Technology has created options for efficiently managing interlibrary loans as most libraries no longer use fax machines to send or receive book chapters and articles; these materials can be scanned and sent as email attachments or even loaded in document delivery software. An example of this software is Relais which allows library staff to send electronic documents to users. Users are able to send and receive materials through this software, marketed by Relais International (http://www.relais-intl.com/). Many academic law libraries use the inter-library loans service to manage the gaps in their collection by giving users an option to access resources not available to them. They also use it to sustain the escalating costs of legal materials, making it impossible for academic law libraries to acquire all the materials they need in their collection. The service is constantly patronized by professors and graduate students.

Resource sharing & cooperative collection

Libraries have been transformed enormously by technology and this has also impacted the various activities in providing library resources. Resource sharing and cooperative collection are collaborative activities by libraries with the same interest. One of the main advantages of resource sharing and cooperative collection is that it helps libraries to save costs by creating a means through which each library benefits from available resources. Through this medium, libraries come together to ensure that financial resources are well managed by supplying library materials among institutions. Lately, libraries have come together to collaborate on and spread the cost of electronic resources as a means of ensuring that institutions that would not ordinarily purchase a database are able to acquire them. This is done through series of negotiations with vendors and publishers. Examples of such collaborations are:

NELLCO (New England Law Libraries Consortium) http://www.nellco.org/.

NELLCO was the idea of a group of law library directors who wanted to address reciprocal inter-library loans services and the escalating costs of library collections in their various law libraries in the New England area of the United States. Over the years, it grew to become one of the most unique law library cooperative collection and resource sharing networks in the world. The consortium is now open to any law library in the world and it has expanded its services to accommodate emerging technologies.

RACER (Rapid Access to Collections by Electronic Requesting) http://spotdocs. scholarsportal.info/display/sp/RACER.

RACER is used to provide lending and borrowing services among member libraries in Canada through interlibrary loans. It is an initiative of the Ontario Council of University Libraries (OCUL) so it is not limited to law libraries. The service allows member libraries to search their catalogues and request materials. Users (i.e. faculty and registered students of member libraries) are able to create individual accounts where they can monitor the status of their requests.

Scholars Portal - http://spotdocs.scholarsportal.info/display/sp/About.

Scholars Portal is another initiative of the Ontario Council of University Libraries (OCUL). It provides access to electronic resources such as e-books, journal articles and data to faculty and students of participating institutions.

SABINET (http://www.sabinet.com/) — This is a subscription-based service that provides access to South Africa legislation and case law. It is one of the more successful stories of access to electronic legal information.

Managing the foreign, comparative & international law collections (FCIL)

In a globally-connected world where the subjects of different nations increasingly reside overseas, foreign, comparative and international law becomes highly relevant. As a result of global migration, legal information becomes an essential commodity for research as well as for answering questions about jurisdictional issues such as marriage, divorce, children, trade, investment etc. For example, Canada and the United States have one of the most diverse populations in the world so over the years there is a great demand for law libraries to build their collections around legislative, statutory, case law and treaties of different jurisdictions. There is a demand among legal researchers for laws of different countries of the world from Europe to Asia, Africa and also in different languages. Another reason why an academic law library may want to build its foreign, comparative and international collection is the demand from foreign graduate students who often need to use legal materials from their home jurisdictions as part of their research.

Another contributory factor to the development of foreign, comparative and international law materials in academic law libraries is the growth and creation of different international organizations which has resulted in new literature. Rumsey (2007) noted that over 30 years ago, the area of foreign, comparative and international law was just a small area. All these organizations have created materials of various types and will have to be made available for researchers. Examples of these organizations are the International Criminal Court, the European Union, Caribbean Community, African Union, and the World Trade Organization.

Building and maintaining academic law library collections in this area has posed a lot of challenges to libraries around the world. In developed economies such as Canada, the United States and the United Kingdom, funding may not be a major problem to access materials from emerging economies in Africa or some parts of Asia. However, it is the other way round for law libraries. For example, in Africa the collection and building of foreign and comparative law collections has a very high cost as a result of currency exchange rates. The library budgets in these libraries are not as robust as those in more developed countries. Many academic law libraries in the United States have a librarian dedicated to this role called the Foreign, Comparative and International Law Librarian. In other jurisdictions, collection development responsibilities are shared among all the librarians in the team.

In some of these instances, the librarians may have connections to foreign jurisdictions and are able to provide expert knowledge for the acquisition of legal materials from these jurisdictions.

Garavaglia (2013) identified nine basic tools for building and maintaining a foreign, comparative and international law collection. One of them is an understanding of the different types of legal system such as the common law, civil law and the religious legal system i.e. Islamic law, Roman law, Jewish law and canon law. The Globalex website has extremely useful readings for law librarians who want information about the legal systems of different countries. Globalex contains legal research guides written by professions from over fifty countries as well as guides for international organizations. FCIL librarians often consult the Foreign Law Guide edited by Thomas H. Reynolds and Arturo A. Flores which is useful as it helps them understand the legal systems of the world and the available legal materials. The *ASIL Guide to Electronic Resources in International Law (ERG)* and the *ASIL Electronic Information System for International Law (EISIL)* are useful resources for sourcing international law materials.

A thorough knowledge of the structure, organization and functions of international organizations such as the United Nations, European Union, African Union and International Court of Justice is paramount. Another tool identified is related to networking. Garavaglia suggests that by connecting librarians with an interest in FCIL, law faculty with specializations in FCIL and graduate students not only with FCIL research interest but who are originally from jurisdictions whose materials you need for your collection. Connecting with a network of students from developing countries where it is always difficult to acquire legal materials will go a long way in assisting FCIL librarians. FCIL librarians should also take advantage of foreign visitors to their libraries who may have information about legal publishers and booksellers in their jurisdictions (Knudsen 2011). Information about foreign, comparative and international law is facilitated by different professional associations such as the American Association of Law Libraries (AALL) through the Foreign, Comparative and International Law Special Interest Group (FCIL-SIS) and the International Association of Law Libraries (IALL). The AALL FCIL-SIS organizes informative sessions and seminars at the organization's annual conference, ensuring that there is a focus on subject matter. The IALL holds its annual conference in different countries, allowing members and participants at the conference an opportunity to learn about the hosting jurisdiction's legal system. This is also an opportunity for members to build their network of librarians, publishers and booksellers. These two professional associations, through their email listservs, assist members in locating and finding difficult international and foreign materials; the activities on this media have been a true networking success story. The websites of these organizations provide professional tips and materials on the collection development of FCIL materials.

Another skill-set that is needed by a librarian responsible for foreign, comparative and international law is the knowledge of one of the major foreign languages such as English, French, Russian, Spanish, Chinese and Arabic. This is because each jurisdiction has its own language and the legal materials will be published in the official language. For example, legal materials from the Republic of Latvia and Republic of South Africa will be written in Latvian and English respectively.

Conclusion

This chapter has discussed collection development and management practices in academic law libraries. It described and identified the materials that are found in these collections as well as selection and acquisition practices. It also discussed collection development policies and their significance in academic law libraries collection development. The nature of the law library collection has changed in the last twenty years with academic law libraries trending towards electronic resources as a result of the global financial climate and developments in legal publishing.

Reader services

4

Reader services

The Reader Services area of the law library is responsible for dealing directly with library users. This is the front end of the library where users come into direct contact with librarians and library staff. They are at the forefront and they answer all queries from users. They represent the library as the first point of contact for the library's patrons and as a result they experience relative interaction with the different library users identified in Chapter 2. In most academic law libraries, the Reader Services department is usually made up of circulation, reference and interlibrary loans/document delivery departments. These departments, in many academic law libraries, are usually located within a close proximity of each other inside the library because their activities are interrelated. For example, a library user who comes to the Reference Desk may require assistance in locating a foreign material that the library does not have in its collection. The Reference Librarian may be able to locate a copy of the book in another university and suggest that the user should submit a request through interlibrary loans. The library user in this instance is a faculty member who is unfamiliar with the interlibrary loan process and there are a lot of patrons waiting to speak to the Reference Librarian. The next step will be for the Librarian to send the Professor to the library assistant who is responsible for interlibrary loans who will explain the process to him. This explains why these areas have to be at close range to each other. In this example, the Reference Librarian will not need to leave their area of the library. The Reference desk (or Information desk in some libraries) is managed and operated by professional librarians. While the Circulation desk and Interlibrary Loans/document delivery are managed by clerks or paraprofessionals. In some libraries the interlibrary loans tasks are handled by staff at the Circulation Desk.

Circulation services

Circulation Service is one of the oldest activities in the library. In the beginning, it was the centre of activity with many staff members retrieving and shelving library materials. Technology has reduced the volume of work in this area and its activities are gradually being phased out with the introduction of with self-checkout machines and flat screen monitors that are used to post announcements and other library-related news. Circulation statistics have decreased in many libraries as a result of newer formats like e-books and other electronic databases. Nevertheless, the Circulation Desk is still very relevant, but the number of staff operating the area has been reduced and they are being reassigned to other areas of the library. Circulation Services is responsible for the following activities in the library:

- Providing checking-out and checking-in of library materials which includes retrieving materials that are on reserve if the reserve collection is closed and inaccessible to library users
- Managing and coordinating the library's reserve collection. This involves entering the records for reserve materials in the library's integrated system. In some institutions, professors request that some materials are kept on reserve for students taking their courses. After the library acquires these materials, the circulation staff in charge of reserves will create a record for it in the reserve folder. This task involves the staff member updating and weeding the reserve collection at the end of each semester so that materials are removed for courses that are not are no longer being offered.
- Opening and closing of library entrances. Circulation staff are responsible for the opening of the library if there are no automatic services to perform this function. They are responsible for playing the closing announcements for the library in institutions where recorded messages are played or for reading out the closing announcement where the announcements have to be made on the public address system. They are responsible for ensuring that all library patrons exit the library and that all library entrances are properly closed and secured.
- Shelving and shelf reading of library. The staff in this area are responsible for ensuring that materials can be easily located and retrieved in the library's collection. They are responsible for facilitating the operation of library equipment such as self-checkout machines, security system, printers and photocopying machines. This includes answering questions and troubleshooting problems for library patrons

Library staff working in the Circulation department are usually very familiar with the library's integrated system which is where the patrons' records are accessed. Depending on the institution, library records are created through the student records when they register for courses in the university. These days all the services in the university are linked together so that students can use just one card to access all these services. The student card is the library card and it is also the card that they use in the cafeteria, bookstore and other services on campus. Just like every library activity, technological innovation and budget cuts have had an impact on the staffing of the Circulation Desk. Academic law libraries have replaced staff with self-checkout machines and the number of staff managing this area has been reduced. Activities such as reserve collection have been integrated to the library automated system. In some institutions the reserve collection is located in an area or room close to the Circulation Desk, library users are able to help themselves and are able to check out materials on the self-checkout machine and this room has its own security system at the entrance. Professional librarians are less visible at the Circulation Desk in academic law libraries and operation of this area is usually carried out by support staff. There is a library manager or supervisor who may not necessarily be a professional librarian.

Reference & information services

Professional librarians are responsible for managing the operations of this department. Their role includes assisting patrons to find answers to numerous questions using a variety of library resources. Their primary patrons are the faculty and students of the law school together with other members of the university community. Then, in order of priority, they are responsible for other categories of users such as alumni, members of the legal profession and members of the public.

The traditional reference desks in many law libraries serve as the meeting point between users and the librarian but individual consultations also take place in librarians' offices. In some institutions, the reference desk has been eliminated for budgetary reasons in which case reference services are available by appointment only. The way services are being provided in academic law libraries have changed and reference librarians may not necessarily have to be physically present at the reference desk. The reference librarian is able to answer questions by email, chat or instant messaging which means that reference services these days are more of a virtual activity. Nonetheless, some users still prefer one-on-one consultations and appointments with librarians so this form of service cannot be totally eliminated. Libraries tend to use a number of social media tools to repackage and broadcast library services and resources. The response to the use of these tools is evidently positive in many law libraries. In short, reference librarians must be able to use social media technology and always crave being technologically savvy!

With the advancement in technology, reference services in academic law libraries have adapted to major transformations by delivering services to their patrons. Compared to 10−15 years ago, many reference materials are now available in electronic formats; for example the Black's law dictionary is available in Westlaw. This means that users don't have to physically come to the library to use some of these resources.

The traditional roles of the reference librarian include the following:

1. Answering in-person enquiries

    This involves dealing with users who visit the reference or information desk to consult with librarians. Questions can range from how to find and locate books and other library resources, learning to use online resources or conducting legal research. One of the advantages of this form of service is that it allows the user and the librarian to build a rapport as well as engage in a conversation that takes place inside the library and face-to-face (Selby, 2007).

2. Answering telephone enquiries

    The telephone became a medium of communication at the reference desk as far back as the 1930s and continues to be used in many academic law libraries. It is often used by users who are unable to visit the library in person, especially students in the distance education programmes who are unable to visit the library in the course of their studies. They are able to relate to someone especially if they are having problems accessing materials for their research, the option of speaking to a librarian on the telephone is faster and saves them a trip to the library.

3. Dealing with virtual reference enquiries

    Virtual reference enables users to access reference services without visiting the library. Virtual reference involves using email, chat and instant messaging tools to answer users' questions. Chat and instant messaging happen in real time. Email allows the user to send reference questions to librarians from anywhere and at any time. Chat and instant messaging are available through different software that allows the user to ask a number of questions from the librarian during an online conversation. One of the advantages of the virtual reference service is that it can be managed anywhere, anytime and it creates room for extended reference hours. Concerns have been raised about security and archiving of chat records from many quarters. The archiving aspect is being addressed by new technological advancements to chat and instant messaging software.

4. Liaison services

Reference librarians provide liaison services to faculty and graduate students and in some instances it is extended to mooting teams and the law review editors. The liaison service allows each faculty member and graduate students to have a librarian assigned to them to help them with their library and research needs. The liaison service is a very common and unique service in many academic law libraries in the United States. At the Osgoode Hall Law School library in Canada, the liaison service was introduced to full-time faculty and graduate students in 2006. Through this service, librarians introduce library services to their faculty and students and assist them with their research needs.

Library instruction & teaching

One of the critical roles of a reference librarian in an academic law library is providing library instruction and teaching. There are many models for legal instruction but the main purpose is to ensure that law students achieve lifelong learning and perceive an understanding of how to find and use legal information. In some institutions, the form of instruction may carry some credits as a separate course or it may be non-credit.

For courses that carry a credit, the librarian designs the course syllabus and course outline, prepares the assignments and marks and grades the papers. One of my first experiences with providing legal instruction was through a collaboration with the professor in charge of Legal Research and Writing to the first year class. I taught the library instruction part of the course. The collaboration involved the following steps:

1. Writing the course outline,
2. teaching my section of the course outline,
3. facilitating practical orientation to the law library,
4. setting examination questions,
5. marking and grading of examination scripts.

Currently, I participate in legal instruction for the first year Legal Process course in my institution; the library instruction part of the course is not for credit. During the library instruction part of this course, librarians work together with the course instructor and provide instruction to students on how to use primary and secondary legal sources. Librarians also use this opportunity to give a brief library orientation to first year students.

Librarians are also invited to the classroom by the instructor(s) for different courses to provide library instruction to students taking their courses. The method and style varies, and the librarian can be given the entire slot or half of the time. Law librarians are often invited by instructors in other faculties such as business, political science and liberal arts to provide library instruction to their students, especially on the use of legislative and statutory research materials. Despite the fact that there is an assumption that legal research may not be as necessary as the lawyering skills emphasized in legal education, lbrarians continue to devise innovative approaches to enhance their role and visibility in teaching and instruction in law schools. However, this assumption is indirectly supported by the law school administrations that continue to slam academic law library directors with budget cuts and library closures, indirectly contesting the relevance of libraries. One of the challenges of providing legal instruction is the research culture of law students in the digital age; they assume that they don't need the assistance of professional librarians because they can find everything online. Studies have proven that many of these students come with an expectation that Google is the answer to their research needs. There have been many advocacy statements issued by professional associations calling for legal information literacy standards. Examples of these are the American Association of Law Libraries AALL Legal Research Competencies, Standards for Law Student Information Literacy 2012 and the British & Irish Association of Law Libraries Legal Information Literacy Statement of 2012. There is the likelihood that these standards will be implemented and adopted fully in academic institutions.

A recent success story is the experience of law librarians at the Emory University School of Law where law librarians were able to expand legal research offerings by introducing five different credit courses. Topics covered include Business and Tax Legal Research and Foreign, Comparative and International Law Legal Research in addition to basic legal research and advanced legal research. These were very well received by both students and administration of the institution based on the number of registration and future offerings in healthcare and technology law. Experiences such as these should be modelled by law librarians who wish to boost the instruction and teaching profiles of their departments. One of the considerations for expanding the course offerings from one to five according to Sneed et al. (2013) was to address the need for one credit course offerings, a very rare policy in many institutions. This model is worth exploring by other institutions where librarians are just invited to teach students how to use the library resources without any participation in testing and grading.

Everyone's experience is different but librarians who wish to specialize in law librarianship will adapt to institutional practices and introduce innovative approaches to their roles in providing library instruction. Bird (2012) suggested collaborating with users to improve information literacy via new technologies that engage them in the process, whether in groups or on an individual basis according to their specific needs. Social networking and Web 2.0 solutions can be used creatively to support courses, ensuring an alternative approach which has the added benefit of being available 24 hours a day online. There are students who will require additional individual, tailored guidance and support to do excellent legal research, such as postgraduates coming to law from other disciplines, with different research. No matter the experience law students bring with them, they need to be equipped with a range of suitable transferable legal information literacy skills in order to be successful users of information in law school and in their profession. Legal instruction is a necessary skill that should provide law librarians with a transferable skill set with lifelong application and relevance (Bird, 2012).

Creating instructional materials

One of the responsibilities of reference librarians in academic law libraries is preparing and writing instructional materials for library users. These materials serve as pathfinders that assist users with legal research. Librarians create topical and subject research guides on various areas of law and they are made available on the library's website. The trend in academic law libraries is using a content management tool, LibGuides for preparing these research guides. This tool allows great creativity and some law librarians have also used it for instructional purposes. See the following research guides prepared by students in a University of Iowa Advanced Legal Research course:

1. "North African Legal Resources" (Maghreb and Egypt) by Hyun-Ki "Brian" Kim http://libguides.law.uiowa.edu/northafrica
2. "Kenya Law Research Guide" by Edward Hall http://libguides.law.uiowa.edu/kenya
3. "Chinese Intellectual Property" by Jee Won "Anna" Shin http://libguides.law.uiowa.edu/chineseip

Legal citation and legal abbreviation

Legal citation and legal abbreviation are part of the language of the legal profession. Legal literature is made up of numerous legal abbreviation and citations. Understanding how to cite legal materials constitute a major skill in legal education. In major jurisdictions such as the United States, Canada and the United Kingdom, there are uniform citation rules for legal materials and publications to be submitted to the law schools and the courts. Even though there are on-going discussions on the relevance of legal citations and why they should be discontinued. Note, however, that in some jurisdictions there are no citation rules; further reading on citation styles is available in *Guide to foreign and international legal citations*. Table 4.1 shows the legal citation styles that are being used in Canada, Singapore, United Kingdom and United States.

Legal abbreviations are the shortened form of description for legal publications such as law journals, law reports, bills and statutes. They vary according to the publications available in each country and they are usually found in textbooks, legal citation manuals and research guides prepared by librarians, especially in foreign jurisdictions. The online abbreviation database Cardiff Index to Legal Abbreviation (http://www.legalabbrevs.cardiff.ac.uk/) provides the meaning of abbreviations or the abbreviations for citations. This database covers Australia, Belgium, Canada, the Commonwealth,

France, Foreign, Germany, International and Comparative law, India, Ireland, Italy, Luxembourg, Malaysia, Netherlands, Pakistan, Singapore, United Kingdom and United States. The availability of an online tool has made the reference work easy and convenient saving hours of searching using legal reference tools and finding aids.

It is part of the reference duties to assist students and faculty to understand legal citations and legal abbreviations. Significant help will be needed by international graduate students who may be coming to a totally different type of citation style and abbreviation. Students in the first year legal research class will also need some help in understanding legal citation and abbreviations. Another group of users who always require assistance with legal citation and abbreviations are student editors of law reviews and journals. These students often need to cross-check the references they find in articles submitted for publication in the journal or law review.

Table 4.1 Legal citation styles

Canada	Canadian Guide to Uniform Legal Citation (Also known as the McGill Guide)	The 8th edition is available in print and online by subscription.
United Kingdom	Oxford University Standard for Citation of Legal Authorities (OSCOLA)	http://www.law.ox.ac.uk/ publications/oscola.php Available in pdf and free.
United States	The Blue Book ALWD Citation Manual: A Professional System of Citation	Both are available in print.
	The Chicago Manual of Legal Citation ("The Maroon Book") Online	https://lawreview.uchicago.edu/ sites/lawreview.uchicago.edu/ files/uploads/v82MB.pdf
Singapore	Singapore Academy of Learning Style Guide	http://www.sal.org.sg/ Documents/SAL%20Style% 20Guide%202004%20Ed.pdf Available online free.

Conclusion

This chapter has reviewed the roles and activities of the Reader Services department of the Law Library noting some practices that are now in place due to the impact of technology and financial being experienced in most libraries. It explains the role of the reference librarian in providing reference and instructional assistance to the users of the law library, challenges experienced in providing library instruction, bibliographic instructional materials and the trends in legal research and writing.

Cataloguing & classification

Cataloguing

Cataloguing is the creation and organization of bibliographic records of library materials using prescribed rules and formats. These rules guide the description of records that appear in the library catalogue. The practice in many academic law libraries is to outsource cataloguing and classification of library materials to book suppliers which means that they arrive shelf ready. And in centralized systems, cataloguing and classification activities of this area are being relocated to the main university library.

The Anglo-American cataloguing rules

The Anglo-American Cataloguing Rules Cataloguing (AACR) were the most widely used among libraries around the world since the 1960s. It was published jointly by the American Association of Law Libraries, Canadian Association of Law Libraries and the Chartered Institute of Library and Information Professionals (UK). The second edition, known as AACR2, was published in 1978 and followed by many revised editions but finally ceased to exist in 2013 with the introduction of Resource Description and Access (RDA). The AACR rules guide cataloguers when creating bibliographic records.

Resource description and access (RDA)

RDA replaced AACR2 effective March 31, 2013; which means that many libraries would have implemented RDA or are still in the process of changing their bibliographic records to reflect these changes. The changes in bibliographic documentation became necessary as a result of the growth and transformation of available formats of library materials, especially digital ones. RDA standards were created to improve upon the on the inadequacies of AACR2 but follow the requirements of IFLA's International Standard of Bibliographic Description (ISBD). Significant efforts and assistance have been made by different stakeholders to ensure the smooth transition of the new standards by libraries all over the world. One such effort includes the availability of a subscription-based online toolkit co-published by the American Association of Law Libraries, Canadian Association of Law Libraries and Facet Publishing representing the Chartered Institute of Library and Information Professionals. Its objectives and principles are available on the Internet - http://www.rda-jsc.org/docs/5rda-objectivesrev3.pdf.

International standard of bibliographic description (ISBD)

The ISBD was created to ensure that libraries all over the world have a uniform and consistent form of describing all their materials in bibliographic records. Its origin dates back to 1969 when a group of cataloguing experts in a resolution to the International Federation of Library Associations (IFLA) recommended the establishment of international standards to regulate bibliographic records. The first International Standard of Bibliographic Description for Monographic Publications (ISBD (M) was published in 1971 and subsequently followed by editions to accommodate serials, non-book materials, rare books and electronic resources. A consolidated edition of the ISBD was published in 2011.

Selected classification schemes used for law materials

Classification following the definition of Raganathan is the organization of library materials in a meaningful manner. Classification allows easy retrieval of library materials on the shelves. Librarians over the years have created classification schemes for the organization of library materials; however law libraries have created their own schemes to suit the uniqueness of the law library collection. Note that some libraries that are usually smaller law libraries have their own customized classification system to address the needs of their collection. The most popular schemes like the Library of Congress (LC) and Dewey Decimal Classification (DDC) are mostly taught in library schools; however it is critical for anyone who aspires to specialize in law librarianship to understand and have an idea of the different classification schemes being used in other law libraries.

I. Elizabeth Moys classification scheme for law materials

The Elizabeth Moys Classification Scheme for Law Materials was developed by the late Ms Elizabeth Moys, a British law librarian. Ms Moys had worked in the United Kingdom as well as in academic law libraries in some Commonwealth countries where she must have encountered the inadequacies in the existing classification schemes that were being used in these libraries.

The scheme uses a dual notation of the letter K or the number 340; in other words cataloguers can use either the alphabet or the numbers depending on preferences.

Here are some of the highlights and distinctive features of the Moys classification scheme:

- Common law jurisdictions are arranged by subject see outline for KF — KN
- Common law jurisdictions have numbers for primary materials - KF (i.e. law reports, statutes etc.)
- Non-common law jurisdictions are arranged by jurisdiction KP - KW.
- Tables I — VIII is a breakdown of subjects allowing the user to be creative with numbers.
- It provides a jurisdiction and topic index which lists countries and can be used as a subject heading.

Examples of Moys call numbers for some law titles:

1. Gower and Davies' principles of modern company law: / Paul Davies
   Call Number - **KN261 .G69 2003**
2. International environmental law: / Alexandre Kiss and Dinah Shelton.
   Call Number - **KC243 .K57 1999**
3. Chitty on contracts
   Call Number - **KN10.A1 C54.29**
4. Encyclopedia of public international law: / under the direction of Rudolf Bernhardt; assistant general editor, Peter Macalister-Smith.
   Call Number - **KC73 E562**

One of the advantages of using this scheme is that it accommodates the needs of Commonwealth jurisdictions and allows for a lot of creativity by the cataloguer or anyone using it. One of the major strengths of the scheme is that it identifies the names of individual jurisdictions in the Commonwealth which are not necessarily available in other schemes; this allows the cataloguer to create specific numbers for titles originating from that jurisdiction. It also allows the use of a dedicated number for the home jurisdiction and the letters KP can be used to classify any publication from the cataloguer's home jurisdiction. For example, many academic law libraries that use this scheme in Nigeria use KP for all publications that jurisdiction. The Moys scheme is commonly used in academic law libraries in the United Kingdom, Australia, New Zealand, Canada, the Caribbean and Nigeria. See Table 5.1 for a summarized schedule from the 5th edition.

See also cheat sheet of the Special Libraries Cataloging services based in Canada - http://special-cataloguing.com/node/1429.

There is a listserv where librarians using the scheme post discussions and useful tips on how to work efficiently. Moys users listserv - https://www.jiscmail.ac.uk/cgi-bin/webadmin?A0=LIS-MOYS-USERS.

Ms Moys bequeathed the publication of the classification scheme to the British and Irish Association of Law Libraries and this group has ensured that there is continuity in the publication of this book and the updating of the scheme. In the process of updating the 5th edition of the manual, members of the Editorial Board called for suggestions and recommendations from law librarians in different jurisdictions who use the scheme. Below is an outline of the scheme from the 5th edition:

Table 5.1 Elizabeth Moys classification scheme for legal materials

K	Journals & Reference Books
KA	Jurisprudence
KB	General And Comparative Law
KC	International Law
KD	Religious Legal Systems
KE	Ancient and Medieval Law
KF – KN	Common Law
KF	Primary materials - British Isles
KG	Primary materials - USA, Canada, West Indies

(Continued)

Table 5.1 **(Continued)**

KH	Primary materials — Australasia
KL	General
KM	Public Law
KN	Private Law
KP – KW	Other Modern Legal Systems
KP	Preferred Jurisdiction
KR	Africa
KS	Latin America
KT	Asia & Pacific
KV	Europe
KW	European Union Law
KZ	Non-Legal Subjects
Appendix	Criminology
Tables	
I	Primary Materials
II	Subjects of Law
III	Dates
IV	Common Law Jurisdictions
V	Courts
VI	Special Legal Forms and Topics
VII	Persons
VIII	Non-Legal Forms and Treatments
Index of Jurisdictions	
Index - Thesaurus	

From the 5th edition.

II. KF modified: KF classification modified for use in Canadian and common law libraries

The KF Modified scheme was adapted by Canadian law libraries from the Library of Congress Class K. It is being used in almost all academic law libraries in Canada. The origins of the scheme date back to the late 1960s through the collaborative efforts of academic law librarians who were proactively seeking a solution for a viable classification scheme for their expanding collections. At that time the Library of Congress classification scheme was inadequate for Canadian and Common Law materials. So in the summer of 1968, the team of Canadian law librarians led by Shih-Sheng Hu of the University of Manitoba Law Library made the decision to modify the already existing number KF in the Library of Congress to fit all materials on Common Law. Their preference was based on a choice to classify common law materials by subject rather than by jurisdiction (Ginsberg, 1988).

It arranges by topic and then by jurisdiction; it only uses the KF together with numbers and so it is quite restricted, unlike Moys which, at the cataloguer's discretion, is allowed to use numbers. Nonetheless, one of the advantages of the scheme is that it highlights the location for materials on different legal subject areas, especially Canadian titles. Members of the Canadian Association of Law Libraries (CALL/ACBD) are responsible for periodic updating and coordinating the publication of the manual for the KF Modified Scheme (note that there is a special interest group of CALL that is responsible for this). See Table 5.2 for an outline of the scheme.

Some of the noted highlights and distinctive features of the KF Modified are:

• It includes special sections to accommodate materials originating from Commonwealth jurisdictions which are not available in the Library of Congress Scheme. These materials include law reports, statutes and parliamentary materials.
• It uses a geographical division (GD) at the end of a subject area or topic. GD classifies and groups materials together, sub-arranging them by jurisdictions. When the GD is used then the form division tables are excluded.

One of the noted advantages of the scheme is that it is expandable and adaptable. Users can exercise a reasonable degree of discretion and flexibility in adding and creating special cutter numbers to deal with particular aspects of a topic not provided in the schedule (Rashid, 2004). The scheme has continued to expand its numbers based on the evolving needs of library users as well as developments in Canada. For example, there have been enhancements in subject areas such as the Canadian Charter of Rights and Freedoms, Quebec Civil law, Immigration, Citizenship and Nationality, Labour, Indigenous/Native law, Taxation and Law of Privacy (Rashid, 2013). There is also emerging literature about this scheme and a user's group which is part of the Canadian Association of Law Libraries CALL/ACBD that produces a KF Schedule which is supplemented periodically.

Blog post for KF Modified Scheme - *http://kfmod.wordpress.com/*.

Examples of some KF Modified law titles:

1. Constitutional law of Canada / Peter W. Hogg
   Call No: **KF 4482 H642 1992**
2. Intellectual property law: copyright, patents, trade-marks / David Vaver
   Call No: **KF 2979 V38 2011**
3. The law workbook: developing skills for legal research and writing / Shelley Kierstead, Suzanne Gordon, Sherifa Elkhadem
   Call No: **KF 240 G66 2012**
4. Sale of goods in Canada / by G.H.L. Fridman
   Call No: **KF 915 F77 2013**

Table 5.2 **KF classification scheme modified for use in law libraries in Canada**

1−8	Bibliography
16−154	Common law primary materials and finding aids are not classed at present
24−37	Parliamentary material
16−49	Legislative documents
50−90	Statutes and administrative regulations

(Continued)

Table 5.2 (Continued)

101–153	Law reports and related materials
154	Encyclopedias
156	Law dictionaries. Words and phrases
159	Legal maxims. Quotations
165	Uniform state laws
170	Form books
(175)	Periodicals
178	Yearbooks
180–185	Judicial statistics
190–195	Directories
200	Society and bar association journals and yearbooks
202	Congresses
220–224	Criminal trials
228	Records and briefs of individual civil suits
240–246	Legal research. Legal bibliography
250–251	Legal composition and draftsmanship
255	Law reporting
261–292	Legal education
294	Law societies, A–Z
297–334	The legal profession
336–337	Legal aid. Legal aid societies
338	Lawyer referral services
345–349	Legal history for the Commonwealth
350–374	History (U.S. only)
379–382	Jurisprudence and philosophy of American law
394–395	Common law in the United States or other common law jurisdiction
398–400	Equity
410–418	Conflict of laws
501–553	Domestic relations. Family law
560–720	Property
566–698	Real property. Land law
701–720	Personal property
726–745	Trusts and trustees
746–750	Estate planning
753–780	Succession upon death
801–1241	Contracts
911–935	Sale of goods
939–951	Contracts involving bailments
956–962	Negotiable instruments
966–1032	Banking
1046–1062	Secured transactions
1146–1238	Insurance
1244	Restitution. Quasi contracts. Unjust enrichment
1246–1327	Torts
1298–1299, 3775	Environmental law

(Continued)

Table 5.2 (Continued)

1328	Compensation to victims of crime. Reparation
1341–1348	Agency
1361–1380	Unincorporated associations
1361–1362	General
1365–1380	Business associations. Partnership
1384–1480	Corporations. Juristic persons
1384–1386	General
1388–1389	Non-profit corporations
1396–1477	Business corporations
1480	Government-owned corporations and business organizations
1501–1548	Insolvency and bankruptcy. Creditors' rights
2971–3192	Intellectual property
2986–3080	Copyright
3084	Author and publisher. The publishing contract
3086	Design protection
3091–3192	Patent law and trademarks
3195–3198	Unfair competition
3301–3320	Employment law
3301–3580	Labour law
4101–4258	Education
4315–4319	Libraries
4325	Archives. Historical documents
4330	Educational, scientific and cultural exchanges
4480–4496	Constitutional law – History for the Commonwealth
4480	General and comparative constitutional law or history
4481–4483	Canada
4483.15	Immigration law
4483. C519	Charter of Rights
4485–4487	Great Britain. Northern Ireland
4488–4490	Australia
4492–4494	New Zealand
4496	Other Commonwealth countries, A–Z
4501–5130	Constitutional law (U.S. only)
4501–4515	Sources
4520	Works on legislative history of the Constitution
4525–4528	Texts of the Constitution
4530	State constitutions (Collections)
4541–4545	Constitutional history of the United States
4546–4554	General works (History, theory, and interpretation of constitutional law)
4695	Public policy. Police power
4700–4856	Individual and state
4700–4720	Nationality and citizenship
4741–4783	Civil and political rights and liberties
4788	Political parties
4791–4856	Control of individuals

(Continued)

Table 5.2 (Continued)

4791	Identification
4794—4794.5	Passports
4800—4848	Aliens
4850—4856	Internal security
4865—4869	Church and state
4881—5130	Organs of the government
4881—4921	The people. Election law
4930—5005	The legislature
5050—5125	The Executive Branch
5130	The Judiciary. Judicial power
5691—5710	Regional and city planning. Zoning. Building
5760—5810	Land and real property
5820—5857	Personal property
6271—6645	Taxation
8201—8228	Indigenous Peoples. Indians. Native Peoples. Aboriginals. Inuit
8711—8807	Court organization and procedure
8810—9075	Civil procedure (includes works on both civil and criminal procedure)
9085	Arbitration and award. Commercial arbitration
9201—9461	Criminal law
9601—9760	Criminal procedure
9771—9780	Juvenile criminal law and procedure. Administration of juvenile justice

(This is an abridged version of the scheme) Anyone interested can contact the KF Modified Committee on the CALL/ACBD website.

III. Library of Congress classification class K

The Library of Congress Classification Scheme has designated the Class K for Law materials. Class K is an addition to the scheme to address the shortcomings of classifying law materials. This scheme combines the use of alphabets and numbers for classifying the different subject areas of law and different jurisdictions of the world. This scheme is one of the best developed and sophisticated despite its shortcomings in accommodating the needs of other libraries; it comes with its own subject heading and it is available electronically on the web here http://www.loc.gov/aba/cataloging/classification/lcco/lcco_k.pdf.

There is a broad division of the countries by continents and further division into regions. See Table 5.3 for an outline.

One of the strengths of this scheme is that it is popularly used in academic libraries all over the world especially in cases where there is a centralized system, the LC comfortably accommodates the law collection in Class K. Similarly, in an autonomous structure, where most law libraries usually share the library catalogue with the main library, the law collection is classified either using the LC or a customized scheme. For example, at the York University Libraries, the LC is used for the main university collection; whereas the Osgoode Law Library collection is classified with the KF Modified Scheme. The implication of this is that where the main library acquires some law titles they will have two different classification numbers and locations. Also, at the University of Ibadan, the law library uses the Moys scheme while the main library uses the LC; they operate a centralized system in which case there will be no duplication of law titles.

Examples of Library of Congress Class K

1. Constitutional and administrative law: / De Smith, S.A.
   Call number: **KD 3930 D46**
2. Reasoning from race: feminism, law and the civil rights revolution: / Serena Mayeri
   Call number: **KF 4758 M39 2011**
3. Philosophy of law: / Mark C. Murphy
   Call number: **K 230 A3 M87 2007**
4. Environmental justice and the rights of unborn and future generations: law environmental harm and the right to health
   Call number: **K 642 W 47 2006**

IV. Swiss Institute classification scheme

The Swiss Institute Classification Scheme is an example of a customized scheme: it is being used at the Swiss Institute for Comparative and International Law Library, Lausanne, Switzerland. It was created specifically for the collection when the library was established in 1982 after many deliberations among experts. This scheme was designed to cover the extensive collection of the library which spans several jurisdictions of the world and international law. It is a systematic scheme divided into six main classes by subject and jurisdiction.

Table 5.3 Swiss Institute classification scheme

Main class A	General Works, general in scope works, comparative law
Main class B	Comparative law: groups of jurisdictions
Main class C	Individual countries
Main class D	Public international law
Main class E	Ancient and religious legal systems
Main class FA	European integration

Examples of Swiss Institute Classification Scheme

1. Public law in East Asia: / ed. By Albert H. Chen et al
   Call number: **BH 34 g PULE 2013**
2. International law: / Malcolm N. Shaw
   Call number: **D 12 g SHAW 2003**
3. Environmental rights: / edited by Steve Vanderheiden
   Call number **A 59 g ENRI 2012**
4. Global minority rights: / Jonathan Castellino
   Call number: **D 17.1 g GLMR 2011**

Conclusion

This chapter has discussed and identified the cataloguing standards and classification schemes being used in selected international academic law libraries. It is useful and helpful for law librarians to have a broad knowledge and understanding of these standards as they may need to be applied at different stages of their career.

Each academic law library decides on the suitable classification scheme that is adapted for organizing its collection; this chapter has identified the Elizabeth Moys Classification Scheme for Legal Materials, KF Classification Modified for Use in Canadian and Common Law Libraries, Library of Congress Class K and the Swiss Institute Classification Scheme.

IT practices in academic law libraries

6

Information technology has become an integral and critical part of the operations of law libraries today. Academic law libraries rely totally on information technology for the operation of equipment, facilities and personnel as well as the delivery of law libraries services. For example, the library-integrated systems rely heavily on technology with new updates being released periodically. Self-checkout machines are a common sight in many academic law libraries which means that they should be properly maintained as they are connected to the integrated library system. Similarly, the library security system is also linked to the integrated library system and must always be up and running as it keeps track of the number of users that walk through the doors of the library. In some institutions there is after-ours access to certain parts of the library for a limited number of users such as graduate students and faculty. Technology ensures that this facility access works properly and allows tracking the number of users as well as when and how they enter the library. With respect to collections, the trend in many academic libraries is to acquire electronic resources to save limited financial resources as well as to utilize reduced library space.

Wireless electronic service is a necessity in academic libraries today. Institutions have this service available for the use of students in different parts of the campus which includes the library. This has resulted in the phasing out of computer labs and desk top computers.

It is now a common practice to buy more electronic journals and books as this will reduce the cost of upgrading and maintaining shelf space. Academic law librarians follow the trends the digital age communicate and provide instruction to their users using IT-related tools. These are some of the developments in technology and how it has impacted and will continue to affect the delivery of information and services in academic law libraries.

How is IT managed in academic law libraries?

The administrative structure of the library will determine who manages a library's IT. Where the autonomous structure is in place the following options are available for managing the IT Department:

1. IT-related matters will be managed directly by the library administration.
2. IT Department of the Law School manages the library's IT.

Both models have their pros and cons, but the most ideal is the first. Using the first model, the law library administration manages all the decisions regarding upgrades of computers, library-integrated systems, compatibility issues with library software etc. Having this option creates a smooth operation and delivery of services. The head of the law library in this instance is usually a librarian whose expertise is in the area of information technology, understands how to manage any technology-related issues applicable to libraries and may have a computer science background and training. In academic law libraries that use this model, new positions are now being created to support IT-related roles. For example, there is the position of Digital and Reference Services Librarian or Systems Librarian. The librarian in this position usually assists with IT-related issues such as managing websites, coordinating upgrades of the library-integrated system and software management, among other responsibilities. This position also supports the all departments within the library. This model is highly practicab and as it helps to ensure that minimal disruptions affects library operations. The IT staff will also be within close proximity of the library which ensures that problems are resolved in a timely manner. Having a dedicated librarian to handle library IT matters will ensure a smooth operation and facilitation of services. Not only will this position bring their knowledge of libraries to the position, they will also be able to apply their information technology skills to handling library decisions.

The second model implies that all IT-related issues for the law library are managed by the Law School's IT department. This is a common practice even though it is highly practical as the two areas are in close proximity to each other but it is still not clear whether the library is given enough priority. Usually the staff in the IT department deal with any library related issues like any other department in the School. They usually need to be educated about library software, the integrated library system (ILS), library databases and other library needs. A way around this model is for the library to work with the IT Department and hire a Systems Technician with some work experience in libraries who will understand the needs of a library from a technical perspective. Where this is not possible, constant communication highlighting the needs of the library and regular meetings between the two stakeholders will ensure there is smooth operation of services in these areas.

Where the law library operates the centralized system, the IT matters are managed by the main library. In instances where there is a separate library computer services department whose staff will be responsible for technology related matters at the law library. In situations where the law library is located outside the main library, there may be delays by the IT department when responding to problems in that location. The response rate will be different if the IT department is in close proximity to the law library.

There are also instances where library IT matters are managed by the institution's IT department. A major disadvantage of this option is that the law library will be at the bottom of the priority list. This may not be the best option but many law libraries may not have a choice in this situation but to learn to deal with it.

Whichever is the situation there is a need for a very strong collaboration between the Law Librarian and the Director of IT Services and his staff. Both areas need to carry each other along at all times especially when upgrades for equipment and facilities are being made. Watson and Reeves in their survey of technology management trends in law schools in the United States found that law schools are trending towards establishing separate IT departments but that law librarians were actively involved in many aspects of technology in order "to evaluate the effectiveness and capabilities of information discovery, preservation, and delivery tools."

Role of the IT department in academic law libraries

The IT Department plays a very critical and functional role in the existence and operation of a law library. As noted, the IT Department may be located either within the law school, the university library or the main IT Department. Here are some of the responsibilities and expectations of the IT department to the academic law library:

1. Maintenance of library computers, wireless service, self-checkout machines, photocopiers, printers, scanners, television monitors and other equipment. In libraries where the computer lab is located within the library, it is the responsibility of the IT department to ensure that these computers are always in good working condition. Periodic upgrades should be scheduled and carried out appropriately with the school calendar and library hours. For example, it is the practice to carry out maintenance and upgrades after examinations have been completed and there is less traffic in the library. It is also their responsibility to ensure that compatible software is available for users on the computers. For example, they must ensure that the latest version or a compatible version of Adobe Acrobat is available on library computers; this is because many library databases use this software for journal articles, which library users may want to access on the computer.

    The IT department is responsible for maintaining library photocopiers, equipment in group study rooms, printers and scanners. Working with the central IT department in the university they will ensure that services are not disrupted from these machines, especially at critical times such as weekends and during exam period.

2. Communication — Both the law library and the IT department engage in constant communication about operations and activities in both areas so it is important that the line of communication be consistent. A breakdown in communication may impact and affect services to students, faculty and other library users. Setting up a Committee with a mandate to facilitate the smooth operation of the two departments that is made up of members with direct responsibilities in these areas is a good idea. The members of the Committee should be the manager of IT services with some representatives of that department, the Director of the Law Library and some members of the management of the library. They can schedule regular meetings which will ensure smooth communication and collaboration between both departments. Discussions at these meetings should revolve around activities and projects related to information technology in the library. The meetings will create an opportunity for professionals and staff in these areas to understand their roles as well as the IT needs of the library. It is the responsibility of the IT department to communicate to the library when upgrades will be made to library equipment so that this exercise can be scheduled for an appropriate time when service will not be disrupted.

As a best practice, members of the IT Department in the Law School can monitor library trends and developments by participating in conferences and webinars; it is an opportunity to network with people of like minds from other institutions as well us learning how other institutions manage their libraries.

3. Maintenance of library website. In some Law Schools maintenance of the library website may be a joint responsibility of the IT Department. Whichever is the case, the IT Department must work collaboratively with the Director of the Law Library by carrying them along in creating the design and writing content for the website. This will involve setting up training and demonstrations on how to use the web design and content management software that will be used by those responsible for these tasks.

4. Additional responsibilities as technology advances. As noted at the beginning of this chapter, technology keeps advancing with new developments on the horizon so the IT Department should continue to work with the library to ensure that they keep up with the pace of these developments. It is important for the two departments to have a mutual understanding in coordinating emerging projects. Building of digital repositories is an emerging trend among Law Schools in the United States and Canada. In most of these Law Schools, the law library is the lead on the project since they keep track of faculty research and keep many of the publications in the library. In order for projects such as the digital repository to succeed, it is important that there is joint cooperation between the IT Department and the law library to take on discussions on the appropriate hardware and software that will be needed. In institutions where there are no dedicated librarians for IT matters, the library will need a lot of technical support from the IT Department for this kind of project. In the process of building a Digital Repository at the Texas Tech University School of Law, Wang noted that it took a lot of effort between the IT Department and the Law Library to initiate the project. This library had a position for a digital information management librarian who led this project.

Integrated library systems (ILS)

Integrated library systems help organize library operations and services. Technological advancements have created efficient library services through different ILS systems, replacing manual services along the way. They come in different modules for different library operations, such as the library catalogue, circulation, cataloguing, reserves, interlibrary loans and serials management. There are various options available in the market and decisions on the appropriate one will depend on the size of the library, the operations the library will be providing, costs and how much the library is willing to spend on acquiring the system. Examples of integrated library systems include: Aleph (Ex Libris product), SIRSI and Voyager. There are now a number of open source software products for open access catalogues (OPAC) such as VuFind, Drupal and WorldCat. The open source option can save costs as it allows for joint and institutional collaboration.

Depending on the set-up in the institution, most academic law libraries share the integrated library system with the main university library. The greatest benefit of this option is that it cost-efficient. If it is shared, the law library does not have to pay for the system in its entirety, and the cost can be spread among the different libraries. A group of libraries in Nevada which includes the Law Library of the University of Nevada, Las Vegas, shares an integrated library system. In a survey of the management of these consortiums, Vaughan and Costello (2011) found that integrated library systems shared by multiple partners hold the promise of shared efficiencies; each library also has a funding formula on an annual basis and the contributions provided by each partner.

Among many other arrangements, Osgoode Hall Law School Library at York University shares the SIRSI integrated library system and VuFind Catalogue with the main library. This partnership works very well and the law library benefits from all system upgrades and maintenance from this package. Most of the law school libraries in Canada such as the Bora Laskin Law Library, University of Toronto, Paul Martin Law Library, University of British Columbia Law Library, Diana Priestly Law Library and the University of Victoria all share their library catalogues with the main library.

In the United States, many academic law libraries share their system while the following libraries have their own catalogues:

1. Lillian Goldman Law Library at Yale Law School has its own library catalogue, MORRIS;
2. Arthur W. Diamond Law Library, Columbia Law School uses Pegasus;
3. New York University Law Library uses JULIUS.

Where there is an independent library catalogue, searches from the catalogue will be limited to the law library's collection. Having an independent system works fine and allows the owning institution to control many functions, but it can be a very expensive venture.

Law library websites

The website of any library provides all the necessary information about the library. Law libraries all over the world use their websites to promote library services and products using different software. The library website is a major part of public service to its patrons. For Plumb-Larrick (2014), the law school library website is a forum to deliver content and services primarily to student and faculty patrons as well as a place for the best advertisement of the law school and its library offerings. A typical website should always be clear, regularly updated and compliant with web accessibility requirements. It is now the common practice for library patrons who are digital natives to be accustomed to using the Internet and websites to research information. With the mobile technology, library patrons want to access resources on their mobile devices, hence the library website should be compatible with mobile devices. With cutbacks and reduced budgets in many institutions, many libraries have replaced their print resources with electronic formats which imply that there will be increased traffic on the library website by users who will want to access these resources from their devices. It is the duty of the library to ensure that users are able to access these resources without any barriers. This will involve both the library and the IT department ensuring that there are regular upgrades to the equipment and software. For example, law libraries are using mobile tagging technology to reach and engage with their users. Russell (2012) in a survey of academic law libraries found that these libraries have used mobile tags not just to engage their users but to complement the mission of the library as well as pointing them to library services and resources.

Law librarians in the digital age will have to understand how to provide library services as well as deliver and manage content through their website. Since many library resources are electronic and can only be accessed through the website, the common practice is now for librarians to develop skills that will enable them to function effectively and efficiently in providing these services. It is not uncommon for a law librarian to create and design websites for library services and library sessions that are taught in the law school. Some law libraries have a dedicated librarian whose responsibility is to monitor and update the library's website. Law librarians in some law schools are responsible for adding content on their library's website At the Osgoode Hall Law School Library law librarians are responsible for adding contents on the library's website as well as making contributions to the library's blog on WordPress.

Depending on the IT model in the law school, librarians should always have total control of the library's website. The Director of the Law Library should be responsible for overseeing the management of content on that page. This infers that librarians must be able to edit and manage the library website.

The most popular website software includes: Drupal, Dreamweaver and Adobe Contribute which are very easy to use and troubleshoot.

The law library website is usually located on the home page of the law school, but libraries have independent pages. A review of the website of selected North America law schools showed that the practice is to have the library tab on the homepage, making the library visible and easily locatable for users.

Social media practices in academic law libraries

Social media communication tools have introduced a global communication revolution that is being felt throughout the world, including in libraries. While it has been proposed that social media tools are highly used by the Gen Y group, the number of registrations on Facebook, LinkedIn, and Twitter shows that these tools are now being used by people of different ages. Social media tools enable organizations to be engaging, responsive, transparent and profitable, according to Kerpen (2011). The implication of these trends for libraries is that users are able to connect with library services and products. Libraries get feedback on their services and the users' comments help to ensure that the institution takes the next course of action. Kerpen noted that listening strengthens the relationship between the customers and services. Engaging with the customer fosters communication and shows a sense of commitment on the part of the organization wanting to know what customers think, how they feel and their expectations for library services. The comments box on social media tools have replaced the suggestion boxes that are found in many libraries. The only difference between the wooden box and the wireless box is the speed at which you have to respond to comments, whether positive or negative. Creating an online presence with social media implies that an organization must respond promptly as fast as possible to any comments from the user.

The social media tools that are being used by academic law libraries include: Blogs, Facebook, Twitter, LinkedIn, Pinterest, Google+ , Flickr, MySpace, YouTube, Wiki and Skype. Libraries, being government institutions, may need to create and develop best practices for staff to guide them on what to post using social media tools.

The common practice is for academic law libraries to establish their presence on social media by creating accounts on Facebook, Twitter, LinkedIn, etc. Through this medium, librarians post news and announcements such as library hours, library training sessions, new services and products that the library has recently acquired. Twitter is used by libraries to announce the latest developments such as an emergency closures, new library hours, events and new titles. Skype is used to connect with library users who are unable to access the library physically, especially long-distance students. It is a cost-saving means of providing engaging library services as well as building the student experience for this category of users. Many libraries upload YouTube videos to market library services which can be viewed by users for varying purposes.

Ahlbrand (2013), in a survey of how law libraries use and manage social media, found that these tools have expanded from the realm of the individual to a platform that connects people in different relationships. The result of this survey also showed that library patrons routinely spend their time on these platforms and that law libraries in general still have a mixed feeling about the use of social media tools. A search on the Internet for academic law libraries present on social media showed the following on Facebook, Twitter and YouTube:

Table 6.1 Academic law libraries and social media

Name	Facebook	Twitter	YouTube
Bora Laskin Law Library, University of Toronto	√	√	
Osgoode Hall Law School Library, York University		√	
Paul Martin Law Library, University of Windsor	√	√	
University of British Columbia Law Library	√	√	
Nahum Gelber Law Library, McGill University	√		
Brian Dickson Law Library, University of Ottawa		√	
Harvard Law School Library	√	√	√
Robert Crown Law Library, Stanford University	√	√	
Georgetown University Law Library	√	√	
Goodson Law Library, Duke University	√	√	
Cornell Law Library	√	√	√
Tarlton Law Library, University of Texas Austin	√	√	
Bodelian Law Library, Oxford University	√	√	

Most of these libraries have active posts while some posts are outdated. One of the advantages of using these tools is that they publicize library activities and resources, and engage the digital natives who can only communicate through this medium. For example, some libraries have featured virtual tours and educational videos on how to use their library resources on their YouTube channels.

Blogs

One of the advantages of a blog is that it 'extends the conversation' between the writer and the reader; it also attracts people to your organization's website. A blog is a website where you can post articles or information that is useful for a target audience. In the case of a law library you can create a blog as part of your main website. Law librarians have their own blogs where they discuss topical issues for education and information purposes. Most law libraries have a blog where they post news items about library services and products, new publications and trends. The most popular blog software commonly used in academic law libraries is WordPress.

Best Practices for a Blog

- Keep it updated with new articles or information as frequently as possible. It is best to set a schedule for posting, such as once a week.
- Make your posts or entries as brief as possible.
- Use images, videos or captions to captivate your audience.
- Have a dedicated staff to coordinate the posts. In some libraries this can be staff working in the administrative department who are technologically savvy and in some instances can be coordinated by the Digital Initiatives Librarian or Web Librarian.

Examples of Blogging Platforms

The following are examples of blogging platforms that can be used to create blogs. They all have a variety of templates that can be used to build your blog.

Table 6.2 Blogging platforms

Name	Website
Blogger	http://www.blogger.com
Tumblr	http://www.tumblr.com
WordPress	http://www.WordPress.org

Examples of Law-Related Blogs

American Bar Association Journal Blawg Directory - http://www.abajournal.com/blawgs/.

Australian Law Blogs - http://amicaecuriae.com/2012/04/28/finding-australian-law-blogs/.

Canadian Law Blogs - http://www.lawblogs.ca/.

Legal Research and Writing by Ted Tjaden - http://www.legalresearchandwriting.ca/index.htm.

Slaw — http://www.slaw.ca.

United Kingdom Law Blogs - http://www.cision.com/uk/social-media-index/top-10-uk-law-blogs/.

The following are suggested best practices to help libraries enhance their presence on social media:

1. Create a social media policy

    A social media policy should include guidelines for librarians and library staff who will be posting with these tools. The policy will contain clarifications and expectations about the kind of information that will be made available on these social media sites. It could be news about library hours, new books, library research sessions, staff news, etc. The policy should include and indicate the acceptable forms of comments that may be posted by members of the public, students and other parties.

    Having a policy in place will help to control and prevent the misuse and abuse of the tools. There have been cases of misuse and egregarious postings on institutional blogs and social media sites so it will be very helpful to have a policy in place to address such issues when they arise. Social media can be engaging, as well as addictive. A clear policy should include and define the number of posts on a daily, weekly or monthly basis. Having a defined period will ensure that the social media pages are updated and not outdated. Samples of social media policy are available in the Appendix.

    Also see the social media policies of the following institutions:
    * George Washington Law Library
    * Ottawa Public Library
    * Toronto Public Library
    * Ottawa Public Library

2. Managing accounts

    The social media accounts should be properly managed. This can be done by identifying a staff member responsible for managing posts. It is a common practice to include this responsibility as part of the position of librarians or paraprofessionals who are in charge of electronic resources. The task of posting and updating information can be rotated among library staff and librarians. Identifying a person to manage the accounts will ensure that there is proper coordination of accounts and updating of the posts.

    The person who manages the account can consult and collaborate with library staff and professionals to get their input on ideas of what should be posted on the website following the library's clear policy.

Institutional repositories (IRs)

Institutional repositories are a common ground for hosting and preserving scholarly publications that are authored by academics in that institution. However, they now commonly include institutional presentations in the form of videos, presentation slides and audio recordings. IRs serve as a medium to share the intellectual contributions of an institution. Rumsey (2006) attributed the following reasons for creating institutional repositories in academic institutions:

1. Management of digital objects, the long-term preservation of research and the posting of output to personal or departmental websites that may lack stability
2. The need to provide mechanisms for dealing with different publication types, multiple versions and relationships (IRs may include datasets, slides from presentations and other media types and need to ensure that metadata for such types complies with international standards to facilitate discovery).

3. Branding and increased visibility, because IR is searchable and registered with search mechanisms.

4. Compliance with requirements for external bodies...

The common trend among law schools globally is to create digital repositories independent of the main institution; but some do opt to include their materials in the institutional repository. The Law Library is usually responsible for the management of the project working with the IT department in making decisions about the appropriate software and upgrades for the repository. Law Librarians are tasked with coordinating and uploading faculty publications, videos of law school events etc. on the website. The digital repository website resides on the homepage of the Law School. Many academic law libraries in the United States have successfully integrated digital repositories into their systems. BePress is the most common software that has been used in some of these academic law libraries in North America. A list of academic law libraries that have created their own IRs with BePress can be found here - http://digitalcommons.bepress.com/institutional-repository-law/.

BePress has been organizing webinars by many of its member libraries on its platform, sharing their experiences on the initiative. The common attributes to the success of digital repositories include the following:

• Support from the Law School Administration
    Many of the libraries claimed that they received financial support and participation from the Law School administration, faculty and students. Building an IR is a huge task that comes with many risks so having the support of the administration will strengthen the focus of the project. This support had a tremendous influence on the collaborative support they received from stakeholders in the project such as law faculty, IT department and other areas in the Law School.
• Collaborative and Planning
    The collaborative support from the professional librarians and library staff was attributed to the success of the digital repository project in some academic law libraries on the BePress platform. For example, at the Washington and Lee Law School Library where the IR project was introduced in 2009, the team leaders of the project engaged and trained library staff on new and unfamiliar tasks. This shows that there is a role for everyone in the library on this project.

The introduction of IRs is one of the exciting long-term projects for any library.

Conclusion

This chapter has discussed the impact of information technology on the provision of library services and products in academic law libraries. Technological advancements have introduced new services to academic law libraries which imply that there is a changing role for law librarians. This chapter has identified some of the trends being used to establish law libraries on social media. Ideas and expected collaborative management of technology between the IT Department and the law library have also been described.

Management & administration in academic law libraries

7

While library schools teach theories of management, administration and leadership, implementing them requires a totally different approach. I should emphasize that not all the theories are practical in the workplace. Management and administration of a law library involves overseeing the operations of human, physical and financial resources. This is a very demanding task and there is no written rule for managing human resources because each situation is different. Depending on the administrative structure, the head of the law library reports to either the Dean of the Law School, the Dean of Libraries/University Librarian, or to both of them. See Chapter 1 on administrative structures. The head of the law library is responsible for managing the human, physical and financial resources of the department.

The typical organizational structure in an autonomous academic law library is shown in Figure 7.1 while Figure 7.2 shows that of the centralized system.

Status of the library director

Depending on the Law school, the position of the Chief Law Librarian or Library Director is either a tenure track or a contract appointment. Usually, this position is an academic appointment but there are instances where it is purely an administrative position. If it is a tenured position, the Chief Law Librarian or Library Director is ranked as a faculty member and expected to participate in scholarship, teaching and publishing.

Role of the law library director/head of law library

The head of the law library is responsible for the administration and management of the law library. This position is responsible for the management of the day–to-day operations of the library. If the status is a tenured track position then they will be participating in teaching and scholarship in the Law School in which case they have a legal background and qualifications. It is a common practice to have candidates for this position who have a advanced degrees such as a Ph.D. candidates for this position combine the other degrees with an advanced degree such as a Ph.D. Some law library directors have participated in teaching courses in the law school while some have facilitated and coordinated Mooting Teams for competitions.

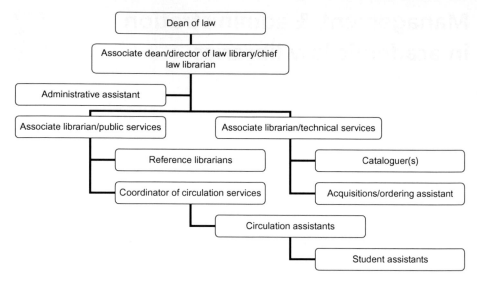

Figure 7.1 Organizational Chart: Autonomous System.

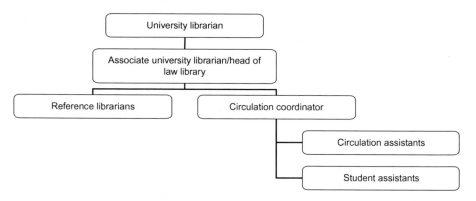

Figure 7.2 Organizational Chart: Centralized System.

Here are some of the common requirements written in recent job advertisements for the position of Director of the Law Library:

- Strong interpersonal skills
- Ability to work in a collegial environment
- Ability to work in a team environment and work effectively with a diverse group of people.

The job description of the Chief Law Librarian includes all of the listed responsibilities and a great many unwritten ones.

The head of the library is perceived by their staff as a role model and in many instances a mentor, and professional librarians and staff will often turn to them for guidance, advice and counselling on professional issues. Hence the expectation is to have a strong leadership orientation and background. Leading by example, making critical decisions without any bias and prejudice are necessary skills for this position. Leadership skills are not taught in library school but they must become part of the responsibility of the individual in this position.

Moys (1978) described the head of the Law Library as one who is responsible to the authorities of the institution, the users and staff for the proper running of the library; they must demonstrate authority and must have and be seen to have a suitably high status within the organization.

The Head of the Law Library provides a vision for the department. They are responsible for setting strategic goals in consultation with other members of the team.

Human resources

The management of human resources is the responsibility of the head of the library. The major responsibility includes hiring, training and the disciplining of librarians, support staff and student assistants. These tasks involve recruiting qualified persons for positions in the law library. The head of the law library is responsible for filling vacancies as and when the necessary. They will ensure that all university human resources policies are followed. In a unionized environment, the head of the library will demonstrate a proper understanding of the collective bargaining agreements when making decisions and recommendations to the Law School administration. For example, in a unionized environment, there are guidelines and policies that are used before introducing certain changes to job descriptions. The head of the law library is responsible for facilitating training programmes for librarians and support staff, especially when new equipment, software or policy changes are introduced to library operations and services. For example, if the library decides to introduce a major change such as the introduction of the self-checkout machines, training must be facilitated for all support staff who will be working in that area. The library can also organize demonstrations for other stakeholders within the Law School, introducing them to the new service and equipment.

The head of the library is responsible for the periodic performance review of their staff and this can be done in consultation with the Human Resources department.

Hiring practices

The method and style of hiring varies by institution, but it is handled by the administration of the law library and the Human Resources Department. The head of the law library is responsible for drafting the job description that will be used for the advertisement. Job advertisements for positions in academic law libraries are usually posted on the institution's website, law library association listservs and in academic newspapers.

The hiring practice for professional librarians is a little different in that, if the position is a tenure track position, it can be time consuming. A 'Search Committee' will have to be set up to complete the recruitment process. This means that the decision is not made by the head of the law library alone, but through the recommendation of a broad representation of groups within the law library, law school and the university. Wheeler, Johnson and Manion (2008) noted that forming an effective search committee is one of the effective methods of hiring the right candidate. The recruitment process in academic law libraries for professional librarians usually takes a longer process and may sometimes take up to a year before a decision is made. But it may be worth the while as this is a collegial environment that requires the best candidates who want to remain in the position for a long time.

The head of the law library contributes to the process of performance review of professional librarians. In some institutions, this exercise is done through committee, especially for those in the tenure track. Where the position is non-tenure, the performance review may be carried out by the head of the library and the human resources designate. Librarians are required to submit the summary of their activities over a period of time. Some institutions have clear guidelines that are used to rank their activities. Examples of criteria used for performance reviews include activities based on:

1. **Professional performance and knowledge** — The review exercise will look at the activities and tasks that the librarian has carried out over the course of their duties related to their specialties. For example a reference librarian will be ranked based on reference activities such as instruction, reference, consultations etc. A cataloguing librarian will be ranked by their duties in the cataloguing section, while an electronic resources librarian will be ranked according to their duties as spelled out in their job descriptions.
2. **Professional Development** — Professional development has to do with research activities; they want to know your contributions to scholarship, your membership and contributions in professional associations and other organizations.
3. **Service** — Academic librarians work in a collegial environment and so their activities should not be restricted to the law library. They are expected to participate in collegial activities such as membership in faculty and university committees for the advancement of the institution.

Jobs advertisements for entry-level position such as an Assistant Librarian in an academic law library usually require both a law degree (JD or LL.B) and a Masters in Library Science, especially in Canada and the United States. Examples of job advertisements can be found on the American Association of Law Libraries Careers Job Page, the Canadian Library Association Job Page and professional group email listservs.

The process for hiring support staff is different from that of professional librarians. The head of the law library will justify the need to hire a staff member for a support position if there is a retirement and a replacement is needed or if there are new tasks that cannot be accommodated by existing staff. There must be proof that the library budget is able to accommodate and support this new position. The hiring is initiated by the head of the law library who passes the request to the administration of the law school, usually the financial officer. There will be no need to set up a search committee as the interview and selection process can be done by the head of the law library and the human resources staff. The head of the library in medium- to large-sized libraries may choose to include on the interview team the librarian in whose area the successful candidate will be working.

Student assistants usually work in the Circulation Department, helping with shelving and information at the desk. The human resources department can help with their recruitment which can be coordinated by the Circulation Manager or Supervisor.

Financial resources

Financial resources include the library budget, funds allocated through library endowments, gifts and donations. It is a common practice for members of the legal profession, especially alumni, to make donations to the Law School with specific instructions that it should be given to the law library. Many law library buildings are named after donors all over the world. The head of the law library is usually included in discussions by the administration of the law school when potential donors contact them and express interest in donating. It is always helpful to compile a useful wish list so that the library will always have a need for any donations it receives.

Library budget

The head of the law library is responsible for planning preparing, maintaining and managing the library's budget. The library budget is administered by the University through the Law School if it is an autonomous structure. If it is under a centralized system, the law collection budget is administered by the University through the main library. The library budget is prone and vulnerable to severe cuts from law school administration. The head of the law has to be strategic, vocal at meetings and aggressive. The trend is for law schools to close junior support staff positions when they retire. The funds are diverted to other areas of the law school.

There is the assumption that all library resources are available online. As a result, this will be an opportunity to free up funds; this is a very wrong assumption as the cost of acquiring electronic resources is not cheap. The head of the law library, whether managed centrally or autonomous, should devise a survival strategy for their budget.

At the time of writing this book, some law libraries have been closed in Canada due to financial constraints.

Physical resources

Library buildings

Part of the responsibility of the head of the law library is the managing of the library's physical resources. The physical resources include the building, shelving, equipment, furnishings — study tables, chairs, computers, security systems, CCTV cameras, etc. The person in this position will have an inventory of these resources, as they will be needed for the valuation and insurance of the building.

In the past 15 years, academic law libraries all over the world have faced a number of 'onslaughts' to their library space due to law school building renovations. Again, based on the incorrect assumption that many library resources are now available electronically, law school administration tend to come to the conclusion that the library does not need as much space at they used to in the past. Library spaces in academic libraries have been taken over by staff offices, research centres and event spaces for the law school. The modern library space being created by library renovations is modern, with an open plan design and bright lighting. It is welcoming and attractive to library users, challenging the general assumption that libraries are places to avoid. Students need to use the library as a social space where they can meet and collaborate between themselves. The head of the law library must justify the need for more study and seating spaces in the library.

Figure 7.3 Modern study space.

After the library renovation in my institution, additional study rooms were added to the existing ones which students are able to reserve online. From my observation, these rooms are always fully-booked from opening until the library closes. These study rooms have flat-screen monitors which allows collaborative work. I cannot imagine why anyone would not like to use this space.

Figure 7.4 Adjustable and Efficient Shelving.

Succession planning

Succession planning, according to Singer and Griffith, is the systemic effort by the library to ensure continuity in key positions, retain and develop intellectual and knowledge capital for the future and encourage individual advancement. This is one management responsibility that many libraries refuse to address but which will always come back to haunt the library in the future. Even though Singer and Griffiths' analysis of succession planning was based on reviews of the public library system in the United States, their observations are universal and apply to academic libraries as well. They clearly describe succession planning as a proactive initiative and a vital tool for implementing a library's strategic plan. Furthermore, Moys suggested a principle that every librarian should remember: no-one is indispensable, and in the event of a sudden illness, or accident, the library should be able to function. Leaders should learn to delegate.

It is important for academic law library directors to develop succession plans for their libraries. There is a need to identify the key roles for librarians on their team. There is a need to always have the library's strong voice and representation at different meetings; if the head of the library is unavailable to participate at meetings, succession planning requires that they delegate and designate another representative to attend such meetings. Strategies like this expose other members of the library team to decision-making responsibilities and leadership development.

The library committee

The Library Committee is an adhoc committee of the law school. The members of this committee represent the different groups of library users, professors, graduate students, undergraduates, representatives of the student association, librarians and support staff. The mandate of the committee is usually to discuss issues that will advance the activities of the library. The role of the Library Committee is an advisory one and not a management role meddling in the operations of the library. It serves as a forum where the head of the library can inform the members of the group about the activities of the department and take suggestions on how to improve services to them. Depending on the composition of the members, the committee has served as a strong advocate for the library in some institutions; they are known to have strongly-voiced concerns about budget cuts being introduced to the library and have called for extended library hours among other changes.

Professional development and networking

8

Membership in professional associations and organizations

Professional development opportunities are available in most professions, especially legal, medical, nursing, accounting, and dental industries. These opportunities are designed to ensure that professionals participate in activities that will help them to improve their skills, expertise and knowledge. Predominantly, this is available at annual meetings and conferences which take place in different locations. With advancements in technology, professional development opportunities are available online through webinars, reducing the need to travel anywhere. Winterton (2011) noted that professionals form communities of practice to share knowledge and skills through personal contacts and through the formation of professional bodies. Attending these professional activities provides an opportunity for a librarian to network and meet other professionals from different institutions. These conferences provide an opportunity to see other people's perspectives and ways of doing things. This could be either through library visits if they are scheduled in the conference program or even through discussions or conversations with colleagues. Winterton (2011) acknowledged the importance of professional development and networking, noting that 'Networking and conference attendance in particular often give an insight into other approaches to law librarianship, perhaps the philosophical underpinnings of our profession, perhaps a good solution to a particular problem, a new way of expressing one's aspirations or a simple new procedure. Beyond the specifics, you get the opportunity to look at your own library services with new eyes, a new sense of perspective that helps to clarify priorities and perhaps unsettles your sense of satisfaction with the status quo.'

However, professional development is not just about attending conferences but about building relationships. I have met colleagues at conferences with whom I have developed and maintained professional contacts and connections. Some have developed into collaborative initiatives where we have worked on different projects, and other relationships have extended from networking at conferences to helpful information-sharing through professional listservs.

Librarians working in academic law libraries are required to participate in professional development activities such as membership of professional bodies and attendance at conferences, among others. Job advertisements for academic law librarians often feature the following — "participating in professional activities at a regional and national level". This implies that membership of professional associations is mandatory for librarians working in academic law libraries. In some institutions, librarians take advantage of the institutional membership which means that they don't have to subscribe for personal memberships.

Membership in professional associations provides the librarian an opportunity to advance the collective goals of the association as well as becoming exposed to leadership opportunities that may not be available in their workplace (Farrell 2014). Librarians are elected to leadership positions where they make decisions on behalf of the members of that association or organization concerning finances, administration, planning and human resources. Farrell (2014), sharing her experience as a representative of her local library association, recalled that in addition to group dynamics and consensus building, library leaders must learn to work with legislators and stakeholders; this is a critical skill that prepared her for her current role as Dean of Libraries.

Professionalism is about being innovative, proactive and creative; peers and colleagues often showcase their work at conferences and seminars; this is an opportunity to identify someone you can collaborate with or whom you can look up to as a mentor. If you're are newbie in the profession, it might be helpful to identify a mentor who can provide some guidance on how to thread the murky waters as there are surely challenges and interesting situations that will come your way, but the solution is not necessarily written down anywhere. Most of the professional associations have mentorship programs but if you're one of those who would rather not participate in the formal groups, making your own arrangement is definitely a good idea.

As an incentive to promote participation in professional development some institutions provide financial support to ensure that librarians participate in these activities. They provide funding for registration, accommodation, travel and professional development leaves. The financial climate in academic institutions has impacted the amount of financial support, and some institutions are only able to provide minimal amounts to their librarians. However, there are means of improvising by applying for financial support available through professional bodies.

Professional associations for law librarians

The following is a list of professional associations for law librarians:

American Association of Law Libraries - http://www.aallnet.org/

The American Association of Law Libraries was established in 1906 and currently has a membership of 5,000 from all over the world. The mission statement of the association is to advance the profession of law librarianship and supports the professional growth of its members through leadership and advocacy in the field of legal information and information policy. The AALL is the largest and oldest law library association. Membership of the association provides members with the opportunity to participate in different chapters all over the United States; caucuses, special interest sections and committees. The chapters represent smaller groups within a state and this makes it convenient for members who are unable to travel to the annual conference. Special interest groups and caucuses focus on areas of interest of members of the association or specializations in law librarianship. Examples of caucuses, special interest sections and committees include Foreign, Comparative and International Special Interest Section (FCIL-SIS), Technical Services Special Interest Section, Student Caucus, Empirical Research Caucus, Committee on Relations with Information with Vendors, and the Diversity Committee, among others.

The annual meeting and conference usually takes place in different parts of the United States in July. Members of the association are eligible to member registration at the annual conference.

Chapters   -   http://www.aallnet.org/main-menu/Member-Communities/chapters/chapter-websites

The following are chapters of the American Association of Law Libraries and they all have grants for their members that will assist them towards funding of attendance at professional development activities such as conferences, workshops, seminars etc.:

- Arizona Association of Law Libraries (AzALL)
- American Association of Law Libraries of Upstate New York (ALLUNY)
- Atlanta Law Libraries Association (ALLA)
- Chicago Association of Law Libraries (CALL)
- Colorado Association of Law Libraries (CoALL)
- Dallas Association of Law Librarians (DALL)
- Greater Philadelphia Law Library Association (GPLLA)
- Houston Area Law Librarians (HALL)
- Law Librarians Association of Wisconsin, Inc. (LLAW)
- Law Librarians of New England (LLNE)
- Law Librarians of Puget Sound (LLOPS)
- Law Librarians Society of Washington, D.C., Inc. (LLSDC)
- Law Libraries Association of Alabama (LLAA)
- Law Library Association of Greater New York (LLAGNY)
- Law Library Association of Maryland (LLAM)
- Michigan Association of Law Libraries (MichALL)
- Mid-America Association of Law Libraries (MAALL)
- Minnesota Association of Law Libraries (MALL)
- New Jersey Law Librarians Association (NJLLA)
- New Orleans Association of Law Librarians (NOALL)
- Northern California Association of Law Libraries (NOCALL)
- Ohio Regional Association of Law Libraries (ORALL)
- San Diego Area Law Libraries (SANDALL)
- South Florida Association of Law Libraries (SFALL)
- Southeastern Chapter of the Amer. Assn. of Law Libraries (SEAALL)
- Southern California Association of Law Libraries (SCALL)
- Southern New England Law Librarians Association (SNELLA)
- Southwestern Association of Law Libraries (SWALL)
- Virginia Association of Law Libraries (VALL)
- Western Pacific Chapter of the American Association of Law Libraries (WestPac)
- Western Pennsylvania Law Library Association (WPLLA)

Australian Law Librarians Association (ALLA) http://www.alla.asn.au/

The Australian Law Libraries Association was established in 1969 with over 500 members. One of its objectives is: "To benefit members and enhance the status of the profession by the further education and training of law librarians, legal informa- tion officers and others". It has 6 divisions across Australia.

The annual meeting and conference takes place around mid-September each year.

British and Irish Association of Law Librarians (BIALL) http://www.biall.org.uk

The British and Irish Association of Law Librarians was established in 1969 to represent the interest of law librarians in the United Kingdom and Ireland. The annual conference and meeting usually takes place in June in cities across the United Kingdom. BIALL organizes professional development activities in the form of training for its members. Members of the association can volunteer on its Committees as well as hold positions on its Executive Council. The BIALL has the following affiliate groups:

- Association of Law Librarians in Central England (ALLICE)
- BIALL Irish Group
- BIALL Academic Law Librarian Special Interest Group (BI-ALLSIG)
- Business and Legal Information Network (BLINE)
- Bristol Law Librarians Group (BRILL)
- City Legal information Group (CLIG)
- East Midlands Legal Information Professionals (EMLIP)
- Freelancers and Solos
- Liverpool Legal Information Group (LLIG)
- Manchester Legal Information Group (MLIG)
- One Man Band / Small Teams Group (OMB/Small Teams)
- Scottish Law Librarians Group (SLLG)
- US Law Firms Librarians Network

Canadian Association of Law Libraries/Association Canadienne de Bibliothèques de Droit (CALL/ACBD) http://www.callacbd.ca/

CALL/ACBD was formally established in 1963. Its main objective is to promote networking, professional development and career growth among law librarians in Canada. The association has its origins from the networking initiative of Canadian law librarians who attended the annual meetings of the American Association of Law Libraries where they converged to have their own meetings. It became a chap- ter of AALL in 1963 and continued until 1972. The annual meeting and conference of CALL/ACBD takes place in May in different Canadian cities. CALL/ACBD organizes a webinar series on different law librarianship topics for its members.

Caribbean Association of Law Libraries (CARALL) http://carallonline.org/

The Caribbean Association of Law Libraries was established in 1984. It is a regional organization established to foster cooperation through conferences and dis- cussions for its members who are librarians working in law libraries in the Caribbean. The annual meeting and conference usually takes place in early July in different parts of the Caribbean.

International Association of Law Libraries (IALL) http://www.iall.org

The International Association of Law Libraries was established in 1959 and its mission is to promote professional law librarianship and access to legal information. Members of this association come from over 50 countries in the world. The association's annual course and meeting takes place in different parts of the world, usually in late September to early October, or in early December, depending on the weather in the hosting country.

International Federation of Library Associations (IFLA) — Law Section http://www.ifla.org/law-libraries

The Law Section of the International Federation of Library Associations was established in 2001. This group was established to provide an opportunity for foreign librarians who are able to attend the IFLA meeting but who are unable to attend other law library conferences. The group participates at the IFLA conference by organizing sessions focusing on legal information for participants.

New Zealand Law Librarians Association (NZLLA) http://www.nzlla.org

The New Zealand Law Librarians Association started as a special interest group (SIG) of the New Zealand Library Association in 1991 but has since become an independent association. One of its goals is to enhance law librarianship in New Zealand.

Nigerian Association of Law Libraries (NIALL)

The Nigerian Association of Law Libraries was established by a group of librarians working in academic law libraries in the 1960s. It is one of the special interest groups of the Nigerian Library Association. They hold their annual conference in different parts of Nigeria on dates that are agreed by members of the executive.

Organisation of South African Law Libraries - http://www.osall.org.za/

The Organisation of South African Law Libraries was established in 1976 and it is the national law library association in South Africa. They hold joint conferences, meetings and workshops with the Special Libraries and Information Services Group and the South African Online User Group.

Special Library Association (SLA) Legal Division - http://legal.sla.org/

The Legal Division of the Special Library Association was established in 1993 as a forum for librarians working in law firms, business and government libraries. The SLA holds an annual meeting in different parts of the United States and Canada.

Toronto Association of Law Libraries (TALL) - http://www.talltoronto.ca/

The Toronto Association of Law Libraries was established in 1979 and one of its objectives is to provide a network for legal information professionals to exchange ideas. The members of the group meet through lunch and learn professional development activities.

More information about law library-related associations is available on the Internet - http://www2.lib.uchicago.edu/ ~ llou/iall.html in a research guide prepared by Lyonette Louis-Jacques of the D'Angelo Law Library, University of Chicago Law School. The website of the International Association of Law Libraries also has a calendar of international conferences and workshops.

Awards, Bursaries, Grants, Scholarships for Academic Law Librarians

Professional development activities such as conference registration or short courses can be very expensiveand many associations provide bursaries, grants, scholarships and awards for their members and, in some instances, non-members. The following are awards, bursaries, grants and scholarships available through different associations for academic law librarians to assist in the participation of professional development activities:

- Wallace Breem Memorial Award - http://www.biall.org.uk/pages/wallace-breem-memorial-award.html
- Wildy Librarian of the Year Award - http://www.biall.org.uk/pages/wildy-biall-law-librarian-of-the-year-award.html
- International Association of Law Libraries Scholarship - http://iall.org/scholarship-information/
- Diana M. Priestly Scholarship - http://www.callacbd.ca/en/content/diana-m-priestly-memorial-scholarship
- James D. Lang Memorial Scholarship - http://www.callacbd.ca/en/content/james-d-lang-memorial-scholarship
- Eunice Beeson Memorial Travel Fund - http://www.callacbd.ca/en/content/eunice-beeson-memorial-travel-fund
- Janine Miller Fellowship - http://www.callacbd.ca/en/content/janine-miller-fellowship
- Lyn Pollack Memorial Scholarship - http://www.alla.asn.au/membership/resources/bursa-ries-awards/lynn-pollack-memorial-scholarship/

Short courses for academic law librarians

Legal Reference Course Materials - http://www.biall.org.uk/pages/legal-reference.html
    This course is organized by the British and Irish Association of Law Librarians. It is a one-day course that introduces participants to the use of legal reference materials and its main targets are librarians who are new to law librarianship.
    Legal Foundations Course - http://www.biall.org.uk/pages/legal-foundations.html
    This course is organized by the British and Irish Association of Law Librarians and the Department of Professional Legal Studies, University of Westminster, London.
    AALL Leadership Academy - http://www.aallnet.org/main-menu/Education/leadership-academy
    This is an annual short seminar program specifically designed for law librarians aspiring to leadership positions in their career.
    Management Institute — http://www.aallnet.org/main-menu/Education/management-institute
    This is also a short seminar designed to provide leadership development opportunities. It takes place every two years.
    New Law Librarians Institute — This program is organized by the CALL/ACBD to assist librarians to develop their competencies in law librarianship.
    Conference of Newer Law Librarians — This programme is organized by the American Association of Law Libraries for librarians who are new to the association. It is available as part of the annual conference and takes place just before the opening of the annual conference.

Publishing

Writing and publishing enables librarians to make intellectual contributions to knowledge. Law librarians over the years have been very productive and creative considering the number of materials they have produced. Notable librarians such as Ms Elizabeth Moys developed and created the Moys Classification Scheme for Legal Materials that is used all over the world today. Law Librarians have contributed to electronic publishing; an example is the Hauser Global Law School Program at New York University School of Law through Globalex research guides and other electronic media on the Internet. Academic law librarians who are in tenure track positions are required to publish by their employers. Some of their publications include reviews of book and electronic resources. They also serve as editors of professional association publications.

Professional ethics

Professional ethics implies the librarian's responsibilities to the institution, to the library patrons and their colleagues. Ethical issues usually come up in the course of performing one's duties and they will have to be addressed. The American Association of Law Libraries has its Ethical Principles, and this can be found in Appendix II with those of the American Library Association and the Chartered Institute of Library and Information Professionals.

The most common example in academic law libraries is the encounter with self-representing litigants who often require extended research and may sometimes need legal advice. The librarian in this kind of situation ought to know that it is outside the scope of their duties to interpret the law, but may assist them in finding the relevant materials. This is when the librarian will remember and put into play ethical principles such as those available from the American Association of Law Libraries.

Conclusion

This chapter has identified some of the professional development practices in law librarianship. It lists the professional associations for law libraries and their activities. It describes professional ethics and its practicality in academic law libraries.

Conclusion

The history of law librarianship in academic law libraries has shown that the profession has evolved over the years from services being offered to the skill sets and training of librarians. Information technology has impacted the operation and delivery of services in academic law libraries. This book has discussed some of the areas of operations in these libraries such as collection development and management, readers and technical services.

It has looked at the various training options available in library schools for librarians who want to specialize in law librarianship. The academic qualification requirements and competencies of librarians working in academic law libraries have been identified. This book has identified the different user groups who will be using the academic law library; their information seeking habits and expectations.

This book has highlighted some of the best practices and activities of academic law libraries by discussing the different models of administration such as the central and autonomous structures. Professional development has been identified as a key activity in the career of an academic law librarian, the book has provided a list of the activities of professional law libraries associations.

Generally this book will assist the novice librarian who is planning to specialize in academic law librarianship to understand what to expect when they are gainfully employed in this setting and as they advance in their career.

Appendix I: Examples of law librarianship course descriptions in the master of library science programs in ALA accredited schools in Canada and the United States

Canada

1. School of Library, Archival and Information Studies, University of British Columbia
   http://www.slais.ubc.ca/courses/coursdes/libr/libr533.htm

LIBR 533: Legal information sources and services – course description

Prerequisites

MLIS and Dual MAS/MLIS: LIBR 500, LIBR 501, LIBR 503 MAS: completion of MAS core and permission of the SLAIS Graduate Adviser

Objectives

At the completion of this course, the student will be able to:

1. Discuss the roles and responsibilities which legal information professionals assume in various Canadian organizations
2. Describe the current trends in legal information services in Canada and elsewhere
3. Recognize the skills required to establish, operate, and responsibly manage a legal information service
4. Apply the principles for identifying, evaluating, selecting, and maintaining Canadian legal research tools, both print and electronic
5. Discuss the basic elements of the Canadian legal system
6. Describe and apply legal research and reference methods, and compare those methods to those used in general reference services

Content

- Basic skills with legislation and cases
- Canadian, English and American legal resources
- Online and other legal sources
- Legal research methods
- Legal reference services in the legal, academic and public library
- Practical law librarianship; running the law library

2. School of Information Management, Dalhousie University
    http://www.dal.ca/content/dam/dalhousie/pdf/schoolofinformationmanagement/Syllabi/
    INFO%206320_W15_2014_12_09.pdf

INFO 6320 – Legal literature & librarianship

Syllabus winter term 2013

Course description

This course provides both a theoretical and practical overview of legal literature
(broadly defined) from a variety of jurisdictional perspectives. It is also designed to
enhance participants' understanding of legal librarianship as a particular stream of
library and information management. Class sessions will include an examination of
the widest range of legal resources, including print and electronic sources. It will
also consider various categories of library and resource collections specializing in
legal literature.

3. School of Information Studies, McGill University
    GLIS 672 Law Information 3 Credits
    Library & Information Studies: The nature and scope of law librarianship and legal
    information sources; examination of the organization of legal knowledge, the legal
    research process, law information sources both print and electronic.
4. Faculty of Information, University of Toronto http://www.ischool.utoronto.ca/lis-clusters
    INF2133H Legal Literature and Librarianship
    Course description not available online
    Faculty of Law & Faculty of Information
    Juris Doctor/Master of Information (JD/MI)

Juris doctor/master of information http://www.ischool.utoronto.
ca/jdmi

The Juris Doctor/Master of Information (JD/MI) combined program:

- Is for students who want to combine graduate studies in information with a law degree
- Is offered jointly by the Faculty of Law and the Faculty of Information at the University
  of Toronto
- Allows a student to complete two graduate degree programs within a reduced timeframe
  of four years, rather than five years, if they were to be taken separately

At the completion of the four-year integrated program, the successful candidate is awarded both the Juris Doctor and the Master of Information degrees.

5. Faculty of Information and Media Studies, University of Western
   LIS 9318 Legal Information
   Course Description
   Sources of legal information and their use including primary legal materials (bills, statutes, regulations, cases), secondary legal materials (journal articles, monographs), and their finding aids utilizing both paper-based and digital sources. Characteristics and needs of users of legal information in law firm, academic, courthouse and other types of law libraries.

United States

1. School of Library & Information Studies, University of Alabama http://www.slis.ua.edu/Course_Des.html

LS 538. Law libraries and legal resources

Introduces the concepts of law library management and the techniques and materials of legal research.

2. School of Information Resources & Library Science, University of Arizona
   http://sirls.arizona.edu/node/868
   681E. LAW LIBRARY PRACTICE AND ADMINISTRATION (3)
   This course will focus on a wide range of issues dealing with law library practice and administration, including but not limited to digital law libraries, collection development, law library administration, teaching legal research, database management, professional ethics and intellectual property issues. Several classes will be taught by guest lecturers, primarily librarians from the law library. (Identical to LAW 681E)
3. Department of Library and Information Science, The Catholic University of America
   http://lis.cua.edu/courses/schedules/#fall

LSC 830 Legal literature

Introduction to major print and online sources of legal information, the bibliographic organization of legal literature, and techniques of legal research; use of primary and secondary sources and finding tools. Emphasis on integrating the use of print and digital resources for legal research.

4. Clarion University http://www.clarion.edu/25497/
   Joint MSLS and Juris doctor at Widener School of Law, Harrisburg campus.
5. University of Denver
   Law Librarianship Specialization

Law librarianship specialization

Law Specific Courses
    LIS 4204 Legal Issues in Information Organizations (3 credits)
    LIS 4374 Legal Reference & Resources (3 credits)
    LIS 4750 Legal Research I (3 credits)
    LIS 4751 Legal Research II (3 credits)
    LIS 4756 Legal Databases Research (3 credits)

Certificate in law librarianship

4374 Legal Reference & Resources (3 credits)
    This course provides students with an opportunity to explore the unique challenges that reference services pose in a legal environment. Lecture, readings, and class discussions as well as practical experience allow students to synthesize course content. Prerequisite: LIS 4060.

6. Dominican University, Library & Information Science http://gslis.dom.edu/law-librarianship
        LIS 788 Law Librarianship
        Credits: 3
        Introduction to law librarianship and the environment in which it operates, including law libraries in law schools, firms and government. Includes an orientation to the legal field, a review of law library operations and administration, and discussion of library service models. Topics include organization of services and space, financial management and technology applications.
7. School of Library & Information Studies, Florida's iSchool, The Florida State University

LIS 5416 Introduction to legal informatics (3)

This course is an introduction to the role of information technology in the creation, management, and retrieval of legal information in the legal work environment, such as the law office and the law library. It examines the use of information technology in judicial administration and other legal contexts; it introduces the student to various definitions of legal informatics while also exploring the detailed structure of legal-information database retrieval systems such as LEXIS and Westlaw, as well as other methods of storage and automatic retrieval of law sources.

LIS 5417 Introduction to legal resources (3)

Provides an introduction to legal literature and to the tools of legal research to create an understanding of how legal information is organized, structured, and accessed in various settings.

8. Indiana University, Bloomington Department of Information and Library Science
        http://www.soic.indiana.edu/graduate/courses/index.html?number=z654&department=ILS

Z654: Law librarianship (3 cr.)

An introduction to basic legal materials and law librarianship. Primary and secondary resources, indexes, digests and citators, specialized research methods, current developments in automated legal research. History of law libraries in the U.S., their organization and administration. The role of law librarians in law schools and law firms.

9. Kent State University School of Library and Information Science
   http://www.kent.edu/slis/courses/index.cfm

Legal resources for non-law librarians

In this workshop, students will become aware of the structure of legal literature and learn to use legal indexes and sources for both case and statutory law. In addition, students will become familiar with the major success of American legal literature, furthering their awareness of the principles, issues, and practices in law librarianship. Finally, the rules of proper legal citation will be introduced.

10. University of Kentucky Library and Information Science https://ci.uky.edu/lis/courses
    LIS 641 Law Librarianship
    A study of the materials of legal research and reference work. Emphasis is placed on the methods of effective research and the actual use of legal materials in the solution of practical reference problems. The selection, cataloging, classification, and storage of materials in a law collection are considered. The specialized requirements of law librarianship and law library administration are treated.
11. University of North Carolina, Chapel Hill School of Information and Library Science
    http://sils.unc.edu/courses

INLS 708: Law libraries and legal information (3 credits)

Prerequisite: INLS 501. An introduction to the legal system and the development of law libraries, their unique objectives, characteristics, and functions. The literature of Anglo-American jurisprudence and computerized legal research are emphasized as well as research techniques. *Offered biennially.*

12. North Carolina Central University, School of Library and Information Sciences
    http://www.nccuslis.org/courses/coursesd.htm
    LSIS 5210. **Administration of Law Libraries** (3)
    The development of law libraries and their unique objectives, characteristics, and functions.
13. University of North Texas College of Information

Law librarianship and legal informatics

Prepares graduates for careers in law libraries, information organizations using legal information resources and information publishers. Enables law librarians to play key roles in the management of legal information in diverse settings.
    See more at: http://lis.unt.edu/programs-study#sthash.8IbaiGdS.dpuf.

14. **Pratt Institute MSLIS/JD and MSLIS/LL.M. with Brooklyn Law School**
    http://www.pratt.edu/academics/information_and_library_sciences/
    dual_degree_programs/
    The University of Rhode Island Graduate School of Library and Information Studies
    LSC538 Law Librarianship (3) Introduction to legal bibliography and research and
    to a broad range of problems involved in the administration and operation of various
    kinds of law libraries. Pre: 502 and 504 or permission of instructor. **Elective.**
15. Syracuse University Library and Information Science
    http://coursecatalog.syr.edu/2012/courses/IST_606
    IST 606 Legal Information Resources and Services
    3 Credits - Offered upon sufficient student interest
    Legal research methods/materials and management of legal information resources.
    Includes federal, state, private, and international legal resources.
16. University of Texas at Austin School of Information https://www.ischool.utexas.edu/
    programs/dual_degrees

Master of science in information studies / juris doctor degree

The University of Texas Schools of Information (iSchool) and Law offer a dual
degree program leading to two graduate degrees: the Master of Science in
Information Studies degree (MSIS) and the Juris Doctor degree (JD). The dual
degree program responds to an increased need for specialists trained in both of these
fields who are thus positioned to help address issues arising from the increasingly
complex and changing world of legal information use, retrieval and storage. The program enables students to earn both degrees simultaneously in three academic years,
including one summer. While the length of the degree program is streamlined, students will still satisfy all of the existing requirements of both programs.

INF 382H - Legal information resources

Identification of relevant legal information resources, efficient retrieval of
legal information, and the role of technology in legal information access.
    Three lecture hours a week for one semester.
    Information Studies 382H and 382L (Topic: Legal Information Resources)
may not be counted.

---

17. Wayne State University School of Library and Information Science

Law librarianship

Recommended Electives:
    LIS 7670 Practicum: Special
    LIS 8110 Government Information Policies and Resources
    LIS 8120 Legal Information Resources and Services

Appendix II: Code of professional ethics*

Code of ethics of the American Library Association

As members of the American Library Association, we recognize the importance of codifying and making known to the profession and to the general public the ethical principles that guide the work of librarians and other professionals providing information services, library trustees and library staffs.

Ethical dilemmas occur when values are in conflict. The American Library Association Code of Ethics states the values to which we are committed, and embodies the ethical responsibilities of the profession in this changing information environment.

We significantly influence or control the selection, organization, preservation, and dissemination of information. In a political system grounded in an informed citizenry, we are members of a profession explicitly committed to intellectual freedom and the freedom of access to information. We have a special obligation to ensure the free flow of information and ideas to present and future generations.

The principles of this Code are expressed in broad statements to guide ethical decision-making. These statements provide a framework; they cannot and do not dictate conduct to cover particular situations.

We provide the highest level of service to all library users through appropriate and usefully-organized resources; equitable service policies; equitable access; and accurate, unbiased and courteous responses to all requests.

We uphold the principles of intellectual freedom and resist all efforts to censor library resources.

We protect each library user's right to privacy and confidentiality with respect to information sought or received and resources consulted, borrowed, acquired or transmitted.

We respect intellectual property rights and advocate balance between the interests of information users and rights holders.

We treat co-workers and other colleagues with respect, fairness, and good faith, and advocate conditions of employment that safeguard the rights and welfare of all employees of our institutions.

We do not advance private interests at the expense of library users, colleagues, or our employing institutions.

---

* http://www.ala.org/advocacy/proethics/codeofethics/codeethics

We distinguish between our personal convictions and professional duties and do not allow our personal beliefs to interfere with fair representation of the aims of our institutions or the provision of access to their information resources.

We strive for excellence in the profession by maintaining and enhancing our own knowledge and skills, by encouraging the professional development of co-workers, and by fostering the aspirations of potential members of the profession.

Adopted at the 1939 Midwinter Meeting by the ALA Council; amended June 30, 1981; June 28, 1995; and January 22, 2008.

This page has long held the **incorrect amendment date of June 28, 1997**; the Office for Intellectual Freedom regrets and apologizes for the error.

http://www.aallnet.org/main-menu/LeadershipGovernance/policies/PublicPolicies/policy-ethics.html.

AALL ethical principles

Approved by the AALL membership, April 5, 1999

Preamble

When individuals have ready access to legal information, they can participate fully in the affairs of their government. By collecting, organizing, preserving, and retrieving legal information, the members of the American Association of Law Libraries enable people to make this ideal of democracy a reality.

Legal information professionals have an obligation to satisfy the needs, to promote the interests and to respect the values of their clientele. Law firms, corporations, academic and governmental institutions and the general public have legal information needs that are best addressed by professionals committed to the belief that serving these information needs is a noble calling and that fostering the equal participation of diverse people in library services underscores one of our basic tenets, open access to information for all individuals.

Service

We promote open and effective access to legal and related information. Further, we recognize the need to establish methods of preserving, maintaining and retrieving legal information in many different forms.

We uphold a duty to our clientele to develop service policies that respect confidentiality and privacy.

We provide zealous service using the most appropriate resources and implementing programs consistent with our institution's mission and goals.

We acknowledge the limits on service imposed by our institutions and by the duty to avoid the unauthorized practice of law.

Business relationships

We promote fair and ethical trade practices.

We have a duty to avoid situations in which personal interests might be served or significant benefits gained at the expense of library users, colleagues, or our employing institutions.

We strive to obtain the maximum value for our institution's fiscal resources, while at the same time making judicious, analytical and rational use of our institution's information resources.

Professional responsibilities

We relate to our colleagues with respect and in a spirit of cooperation.

We distinguish between our personal convictions and professional duties and do not allow our personal beliefs to interfere with the service we provide.

We recognize and respect the rights of the owner and the user of intellectual property.

We strive for excellence in the profession by maintaining and enhancing our own knowledge and skills, by encouraging the professional development of co-workers, and by fostering the aspirations of potential members of the profession.

Ethical principles background information

The Special Committee on Ethics was appointed in 1997 by then-President Judy Meadows for the purpose of reviewing the Association's Code of Ethics and proposing any revisions necessary. The Code of Ethics incorporates by reference the ALA Code of Ethics which has been revised twice since the AALL Code was adopted. The Special Committee followed a previous AALL taskforce and other groups in studying possible revisions to the AALL Code of Ethics.

The Special Committee studied the current Code of Ethics and determined that the Code should be replaced. The Committee examined in detail the codes of ethics of other professional associations, including sister library organizations, and wrote articles for *AALL Spectrum* throughout the past year which called attention to the Committee's efforts and mission.

The Committee met in Chicago in May 1998 and drafted much of the proposed Ethical Principles. Committee members added portions later, and the final draft was circulated and discussed extensively at the Annual Meeting in Anaheim. Registrants received copies in their packets, they could record their responses on a flipchart located by the entrance to the Exhibit Area, and they could voice their concerns at the second portion of the Open Forum. Further, members with e-mail addresses received a copy of the proposed Ethical Principles in a message broadcast from AALL Headquarters. The Committee received several responses and considered them carefully. As a result, the Committee revised some of what was circulated to the membership and brought these Ethical Principles to the Executive Board at its

Fall 1998 meeting with the suggestion that they be submitted to the AALL member-
ship for approval. The Ethical Principles were submitted to the membership in
March 1999 and approved by an overwhelming majority vote.
   Submitted by: J. Wesley Cochran, Chair
   Ethics (Special Committee)

cilip Chartered Institute of Library and Information Professionals

Code of professional practice for library and information professionals

This Code applies the ethical principles to the different groups and interests to
which CILIP members must relate. The Code also makes some additional points
with regard to professional behaviour. The principles and values will differ in their
relative importance according to context.

A. Personal responsibilities

*People who work in the information profession have personal responsibilities which
go beyond those immediately implied by their contract with their employers or clients.
Members should therefore:*

1. Strive to attain and continue to develop the highest personal standard of professional
   knowledge and competence.
2. Ensure they are competent in those branches of professional practice in which qualifications and/or experience entitle them to engage by keeping abreast of developments
   in their areas of expertise.
3. Claim expertise in areas of library and information work or in other disciplines only
   where their skills and knowledge are adequate.
4. Refrain from any behaviour in the course of their work which might bring the information profession into disrepute.

B. Responsibilities to information and its users

*The behaviour of professionals who work with information should be guided by a
regard for the interests and needs of information users. People working in the information profession also need to be conscious that they have responsibility for a growing heri-
tage of information and data, irrespective of format. This includes works of the
imagination as well as factual data. Members should therefore:*

1. Ensure that information users are aware of the scope and remit of the service being
   provided.
2. Make the process of providing information, and the standards and procedures govern-
   ing that process, as clear and open as possible.
3. Avoid inappropriate bias or value judgements in the provision of services.

4. Protect the confidentiality of all matters relating to information users, including their enquiries, any services to be provided, and any aspects of the users' personal circumstances or business.

5. Carry out and use research involving users (e.g. surveys of needs) in a responsible manner, ensuring that best practice is followed as set out in law or in codes of conduct recommended by research organisations (e.g. universities) or professional bodies.

6. Deal fairly with the competing needs of information users, and resolve conflicting priorities with due regard for the urgency and importance of the matters being considered.

7. Deal promptly and fairly with any complaints from information users, and keep them informed about progress in the handling of their complaints.

8. Ensure that the information systems and services for which they are responsible are the most effective, within the resources available, in meeting the needs of users.

9. Ensure that the materials to which they provide access are those which are most appropriate to the needs of legitimate users of the service.

10. Defend the legitimate needs and interests of information users, while upholding the moral and legal rights of the creators and distributors of intellectual property.

11. Respect the integrity of information sources, and cite sources used, as appropriate.

12. Show an appropriate concern for the future information needs of society through the long-term preservation and conservation of materials as required, as well as an understanding of proper records management.

C. **Responsibilities to colleagues and the information community**

The personal conduct of information professionals at work should promote the profession in the best possible manner at all times. Members should therefore:

1. Act in ways that promote the profession positively, both to their colleagues and to the public at large.

2. Afford respect and understanding to other colleagues, including those in other professions, and acknowledge their ideas, contributions and work, wherever and whenever appropriate.

3. Refer to colleagues in a professional manner and not discredit or criticise their work unreasonably or inappropriately.

4. When working in an independent capacity, conduct their business in a professional manner that respects the legitimate rights and interests of others.

5. Encourage colleagues, especially those for whom they have a line-management responsibility, to maintain and enhance their professional knowledge and competence.

6. Ensure that any member of staff to whom a task is delegated has the knowledge and skills necessary to undertake that task effectively and efficiently.

7. Share, where possible, results of research and development projects they have been involved in to help encourage best practice across the profession and enable colleagues to improve the services they provide.

8. Refrain from ascribing views to, or speaking on behalf of, CILIP, unless specifically authorised to do so.

9. Report significant breaches of this Code to the appropriate authorities.[1]

---

[1] The appropriate authority will vary depending on the context of the case. It may be CILIP, the employer, a regulatory body or an officer managing the 'whistle-blowing' procedure or some other body. It is not possible to be prescriptive.

D. Responsibilities to society

One of the distinguishing features of professions is that their knowledge and skills are at the service of society at large, and do not simply serve the interests of the immediate customer. Members should therefore:

1. Consider the public good, both in general and as it refers to particular vulnerable groups, as well as the immediate claims arising from their employment and their professional duties.
2. Promote equitable access for all members of society to public domain information of all kinds and in all formats.
3. Promote the necessary skills and knowledge amongst users to become effective independent learners and researchers.
4. Strive to achieve an appropriate balance within the law between demands from information users, the need to respect confidentiality, the terms of their employment, the public good and the responsibilities outlined in this Code.
5. Encourage and promote wider knowledge and acceptance of, and wider compliance with, this Code, both among colleagues in the information professions and more widely among those whom we serve.

E. Responsibilities as employees

Members who are employed have duties that go beyond the immediate terms of their employment contract. On occasion these may conflict with the immediate demands of their employer but be in the broader interest of the public and possibly the employer themselves.[2] Members should therefore:

1. Develop a knowledge and understanding of the organisation in which they work and use their skills and expertise to promote the legitimate aims and objectives of their employer.
2. Avoid engaging in unethical practices during their work and bring to the attention of their employer any concerns they may have concerning the ethics or legality of specific decisions, actions or behaviour at work.

CILIP, 2004, amended 2012.

---

[2] It is recognised that sometimes Members, acting as a representative of employers, have to make decisions that may impact adversely on levels of service or the employment of staff.

This is not in itself unethical behaviour but there might be circumstances in which it could be — the lawfulness of the action or the way it is managed, for instance.

Appendix III: AALL social media policy

Approved by the Executive Board November 1, 2013, Tab 16
These are the official policies for social media use on behalf of the American Association of Law Libraries (AALL). Social Media is defined as any website or application that enables individuals to post and share content that others can view and also share. Social Media tools include, but are not limited to, social-networking sites, social sharing sites, social bookmarking, micro-blogging tools, wikis, and blogs, among other tools.

The policy below has been developed to assist you in using social media effectively. It covers what is recommended, expected and required when staff and the Executive Board discuss Association-related topics, whether at work or on their own time, in a public forum.

This policy applies to:

All Staff and Executive Board members of the American Association of Law Libraries (the "Association"). It applies to conduct by or between co-workers, managers/supervisors, employees, consultants, independent contractors, customers, vendors, suppliers, or any other persons who do business with the Association.

Policy for social media site administrators:

If you are responsible for an existing or newly approved AALL-branded social media site, please refer to the additional Social Media Policies for Site Administrators.

Guidelines:

The prevalence of Social Media has blurred the lines between public and private, personal and professional. By identifying yourself as having an affiliation with AALL (e.g., listing AALL as your employer), you are creating perceptions about AALL and your expertise. We expect all who participate in social media on behalf of AALL — or whose participation in a social media activity might reasonably be interpreted as representing or reflecting upon AALL — to understand and follow these policies.

1. **Personally responsible for content** — You are personally responsible for the content you publish online. While, in general, what an employee does outside of work is his or her affair, activities in or outside of work that affect job performance, the performance of others, or the Association's interests, do fall within the focus of this policy. Do not post anything that could compromise your professional image, along with your colleagues or AALL.
2. **Proprietary or confidential information** — If an individual publishes content related to work or subjects associated with the Association online, the individual needs to ensure that the content is not proprietary or confidential to the Association. Ask permission to publish or report on conversations that are meant to be private or internal to the Association.
3. **Participant** — Although not as an official representative of the Association, participation in blogs, discussion forums, etc. is encouraged. Bring value when commenting. Stick to your area of expertise and provide unique, individual perspectives. Be informative and interesting; check facts and figures. If you see something interesting, valuable, or relevant, share it.
4. **Social networks and company affiliation** — Be aware of your association with AALL while online. If you identify yourself as an Association employee or Board Member, ensure your profile and related content is consistent with how you wish to present yourself with colleagues and members. Be mindful of the forum/venue you participate in as well; be sure it is consistent with the values and business conduct guidelines of the Association.
5. **Use a disclaimer** — Whether you publish to a blog or some other form of social media, make it clear that what you say there is representative of your views and opinions and not necessarily the views and opinions of AALL. At a minimum in your own blog, you should include the following standard disclaimer: "The postings on this site are my own and don't necessarily represent American Association of Law Libraries positions, strategies or opinions."
6. **Think before you post** — The internet is not anonymous and does not forget. Search engines can turn up posts years after the publication date. Comments can be forwarded or copied. Archival systems save information even if you delete a post. If you feel angry or passionate about a subject, it's wise to delay posting until you are calm and clear-headed.
7. **References to members** — Don't cite or reference members without their approval. Link back to the source, when possible, if you do make a reference.
8. **Inaccurate information** — Be an ambassador, if you see misrepresentations made about AALL online, contact the Director of Membership Marketing and Communications. They will work with the Board and the Executive Director to get inaccurate content about the Association corrected. Be the first to correct your own mistakes, and don't alter previous posts without indicating that you have done so.
9. **Copyright** — Accurately attribute material that is not your own. Respect copyright, fair use and financial disclosure laws.
10. **Acceptable conduct** — Respect your audience. Don't engage in any conduct that would not be acceptable in the Association's workplace. You should also show proper consideration for others' privacy and for topics that may be considered sensitive, such as politics and religion. Consider the audience. It can include current or potential members, and current/past/future staff. Use privacy settings to restrict personal information on otherwise public sites.
11. **Professional commitments** — Ensure that your online activities do not interfere with your job or commitments to members.

Responsibility for the enforcement of this policy:

Department directors will be responsible for compliance. As with all Association policies, compliance will be subject to review by the Executive Director, Executive Board, and Human Resources. Any exception to this policy requires the express written approval of the Executive Director and the Executive Board.

Violation of this policy:

Violation of this policy and any related procedures may result in disciplinary action, up to and including termination of employment. The Association reserves the right to remove content from an employee's post made while representing the Association if the post is in violation of the policy outlined above.

General statement:

As with all policies and procedures, the Association reserves the right to modify, revise, discontinue or terminate this policy at any time without prior notice.

Please see related policies for more information:

Social media policies for site administrators

If you are responsible for an existing or newly approved AALL-branded social media site including, but not limited to, Facebook page, Twitter account, LinkedIn group, YouTube channel, or blog, these policies are designed to help you and the entire Association succeed. These policies are in addition to the AALL Social Media Policy.

1. **Register with the Director of Membership Marketing and Communications** — Be added to the inventory of social media sites and receive important information about AALL's social media activity. Only registered sites will be allowed to use the AALL affiliation.
2. **Stay Current** — You are expected to maintain your site and update it regularly.
3. **Monitor and moderate posts as appropriate** — Review content prior to posting when necessary, but encourage a free flow of ideas as much as possible. Monitor the site to learn the needs of your fans/followers and moderate accordingly. Do not allow anonymous postings.
4. **Include your contact information** — Make it easy for members to contact you to report inappropriate content or to connect with AALL.
5. **Have a succession plan** — Maintain at least two administrators to cover any instances when someone will no longer be able to participate.

Appendix IV: Legal publishers & booksellers

The following is a list of legal publishers and booksellers. Note that this is not an exhaustive list but it can be helpful for collection development responsibilities.

Bloomberg BNA — http://www.bloomberg.com
Gaunt Publishing — http://www.gaunt.com/publishers.html
Gale — http://gdc.gale.com/
HeinOnline — http://home.heinonline.org/
Cambridge University Press — http://www.cambridge.org
Emond Montgomery Publications — http://www.emp.ca/
LexisNexis — They are located in different parts of the world
Meyer Boswell Books, Inc — http://www.meyerbos.com/cgi/meyerbo2/perlshop.cgi? thispage=/home/WWW_pages/meyerbo2/meyerbos.com/home.html
Thomson Reuters — http://www.thomsonreuters.com
Irwin Law Publishers — http://www.irwinlaw.com/
Juta Law — http://www.jutalaw.co.za
Justis — http://www.justis.com
Maritime Law Book — http://mlb.nb.ca/html/resources-law-books.html
Nigerian Law Publications Ltd. — http://www.nigerianlawpublications.com/aboutus.html
Oxford University Press — http://global.oup.com/?cc=ca
The Law Book Exchange — http://www.lawbookexchange.com/
The Incorporated Council for Law Reporting of England & Wales — http://www.iclr.co.uk/products/iclr-online/
Toma Micro Publishers — http://www.tomalegalretrieve.org/pages/home-page.php
MIJ Professional Publishers — http://mijprofessionalpublishers.com/home/
Safari Books (Formerly Spectrum Books) — http://www.safaribooksng.com/index.php
vLex Global — http://us.vlex.com/
Wildy, Simmons & Hill Publishing — http://www.wildy.com/about-wsh
Wolters Kluwer — http://www.wolterskluwer.com
Routledge Taylor & Francis Group — http://www.routledge.com/law/
University Press

Most universities in the United Kingdom and North America own publishing companies and they usually publish law titles. Below is a list of some of them:

UBC Press — http://www.ubcpress.com
Harvard University Press — http://www.hup.harvard.edu
University of Toronto Press — http://www.utpress.utoronto.ca/

Bibliography

2013 Law Library Guide, Yale Law Library. May 8, 2014. <http://library.law.yale.edu/2013-law-library-guide>.

Accreditation Council of Trinidad and Tobago Act. Tran. Ministry of Legal Affairs Trinidad & Tobago. Cap 39:06 8(1), 2012.

Agboola, A.T., 2001. Non-tenured leadership appointments in Nigerian university libraries: problems and prospects. Library Management 22 (6/7), 288–296.

Agrawal, N.K., 2013. Training in FCIL librarianship for tomorrow's world. Law Libr. J. 105, 199.

Ahlbrand, A., 2013. The "social" side of law libraries: how are libraries using and managing social media? AALL Spectrum 117 (5), 12.

Alvite, L., Barraionuevo, L., 2011. Libraries for Users: Services in Academic Libraries. Chandos Publishing, Oxford.

American Bar Association, 2012–2013. ABA Standards and rules of procedure for approval of law schools. <http://www.americanbar.org/groups/legal_education/resources/standards.html>.

American Bar Association, 2012–2013. ABA - Approved law schools. July 14, 2013. <http://www.americanbar.org/groups/legal_education/resources/aba_approved_law_schools.html>.

Association of American Law Schools Bylaws. <http://www.aals.org/about_handbook_bylaws.php>.

Bernstein, M.P., Cannan, J., 2013. Evolution in American legal education: implications for academic law collections. In: Holder, S. (Ed.), Library Collection Development for Professional Programs: Trends and Practices. Information Science Reference, Hershey, PA, p. 53.

Berring, R.C., 2013. The education of the twentieth-century law librarian. Legal Reference Services Quarterly 32 (1–2), 1.

Bird, R., 2011. Legal information literacy. In: Danner, R.A., Winterton, J. (Eds.), Handbook of Legal Information Management. Ashgate Publications, Farnham, Surrey, p. 115.

Brock, C., 1974. Law libraries and law librarians: a revisionist theory. Or more than you ever wanted to know. Law Libr. J. 67.

Byrum, J.D., 2000. The birth and re-birth of the ISBDs: process and procedures for creating and revising the international standard bibliographic descriptions. 66th IFLA Council and General Conference 13–18. IFLA, Jerusalem, Israel, Netherlands.

Cadmus, F., 2009. Making the leap to management tips for the aspiring and new manager. Trends in Law Library Management and Technology 19.

Cadmus, F., 2012. Happiness at work: rules for employee satisfaction and engagement. Trends in Law Library Management and Technology 22.

Cadmus, F., Kauffman, B., 2010. The recession mounts the ivory tower: how the Lillian Goldman law library at Yale has met the challenges posed by a declining economy. Librarian Scholarship Series. Paper 2.

Courtney, S., 2007. The evolution of the reference interview. Legal Ref. Serv. Q. 26 (1–2), 35.

Crane, M.B., 1993. The New England law library consortium. Law Libr. J. 83.

Danner, R.A., 2003. Contemporary and future directions in American legal research: responding to the threat of the available. International Journal of Legal Information 31, 217.

Demers, A.L., 2012. Working in a University Library. Legal Information Specialists: A Guide to Launching and Building Your Career. LexisNexis Canada Inc., Markham, Ontario.

Farrell, M., 2014. Leadership reflections: leadership development through service. Journal of Library Administration 54 (4), 308.

Garavaglia, B. Collection development policies and other basic tools for building a foreign and international law collection Globalex: Foreign Law Research. August 2013. January 14, 2014. <http://www.nyulawglobal.org/globalex/International_Foreign_Collection_Development1.htm>.

General Assembly. Convention on the rights of persons with disabilities. Tran. United Nations. 61/106 New York: 2007.

Ginsberg, J., 1988. Classification schemes used in law libraries in Canada feature. Canadian Association of Law Libraries Newsletter Bulletin 13.

Gregory, V.L., 2011. Collection Development and Management for 21st Century Library Collections: An Introduction. Neal-Schuman Publishers, New York.

Healey, P., 2008. Professional Liability Issues for Librarians and Information Professionals. Neal-Schuman Publishers, New York.

Healey, P.D., 2014. Legal Reference for Librarians. American Library Association, Chicago.

Hill, J., Li, H., Macheak, C., 2013. Current practices in distance learning library services at Urban and Metropolitan universities. Journal of Library & Information Services in Distance Learning 7 (3), 313.

Hirsch, C., 2012. The rise and fall of academic law library collection standards. Legal Ref. Serv. Q. 31 (1).

Holloway, K., 2011. Outreach to distance students: a case study of a new distance librarian. Journal of Library & Information Services in Distance Learning 5, 1.

International Federation of Library Associations About the ISBD review about the ISBD review group. 2014. <http://www.ifla.org/about-the-isbd-review-group>.

IFLA Law libraries section annual report 2007 plus report 2001−2006. <http://www.ifla.org/files/assets/law-libraries/annual-reports/2001-2007-en.pdf>.

Jeffries, J., 1989. Law librarianship in the United Kingdom: preparation, the profession, and the British and Irish association of law librarians. Law Libr. J. 81.

Kerpen, D., 2011. Likeable Social Media. Soundview Executive Book Summaries, Norwood, Mass.

Knight, F.T., 2002. Future of KF modified in Canadian law libraries, the reports. Can. Law Libr. 27.

Knight, F.T., 2009. KF modified and the classification of Canadian common law. Can. Law Libr. Rev. 34.

Knudsen, H., 2011. Collection building: foreign, comparative and international law in print. In: Danner, R.A., Winterton, J. (Eds.), Handbook of Legal Information Management. Ashgate Publications, Farnham, Surrey, p. 247.

Lerdal, S.N., 2006. Evidence-based librarianship: opportunity for law librarians general article. Law Libr. J. 98.

Lewis, S.H., 2002. A three-tiered approach to faculty services librarianship in the law school environment. Law Libr. J. 94.

Mersky, R., 1976. Bicentennial history of American law libraries. Law Libr. J. 69.

Milles, J.G., 2004. Leaky boundaries and the decline of the autonomous law school library. Law Libr. J. 96.

Moys, E.M., 1987. General administration. In: Moys, E. (Ed.), Manual of Law Librarianship, second ed. British and Irish Association of Law Librarians, Boston, MA, p. 595.

New York University School of Law, 2009. Guide to Foreign and International Legal Citations, second ed. Aspen Publishers, New York.

Olson, K.C., 2013. Legal Research in a Nutshell, eleventh ed. West Publishing, St. Paul, MN.

Ontario Universities Council Ontario universities council on quality assurance.

Pickett, C., 2011. Revisiting an abandoned practice: the death and resurrection of collection development policies. Collection Management 36 (3).

Ranganathan, S.R., 1964. The Five Laws of Library Science. Asia Pub. House, Bombay.

Roberts, D., Hunter, D., 2011. New library, new librarian, new student: using libguides to reach the virtual student. Journal of Library & Information Services in Distance Learning 5 (1—2), 67.

Rumsey, M., 2007. Foreign, comparative and international law librarianship. Law Librarianship in the Twenty-First Century. Scarecrow Press, Lanham, MD.

Russell, A., Spina, C., 2012. Law libraries linking data to mobile devices - save patrons' time and stay hip. AALL Spectrum 106, 16.

Sannwald, W.W. (Ed.), 2001. Checklist of Library Building Design Considerations, fourth ed. American Library Association, Chicago.

Slade, A.L. Research on library services for distance learning: an international perspective. Journal of Library & Information Services in Distance Learning 1, 1.

Smith, A.T.H., 2010. Glanville Williams: Learning the Law. Sweet and Maxwell, London.

Smith, S.R., 2006. The best system of accreditation in America. Syllabus 38 (1).

Sneed, T., Flick, A., Christian, E., 2013. Changing the law library instructional curriculum, part I: the first year and student demographics. Trends in Law Library Management and Technology 23.

Sneed, T., Flick, A., Christian, E., 2013. Changing the law library instructional curriculum, part 2: a different schedule and the management perspective. Trends in Law Library Management and Technology 23.

Wang, F., 2011. Building an open Source I the history of law librarianship in academic law libraries nstitutional repository at a small law school library: is it realistic or unattainable? Information Technology and Libraries 30 (2).

Watson, C., Reeves, L., 2011. Technology management trends in law schools. Law Libr. J. 110 (3).

Wheeler, R., Johnson, N.P., Manion, T.K., 2008. Choosing the top candidate: best practices in academic law library hiring. Law Libr. J. 100 (1).

Index